W9-BEG-672

CHAPTER 2

The Foundation Of It All

ספר מסילת ישרים - פרק א

יְסוֹד הַחֲסִידוּת וְשֹׁרֶשׁ הָעֲבוֹדָה הַתְּמִימָה הוּא -
שֶׁיִּתְבָּרֵר וְיִתְאַמֵּת אֵצֶל הָאָדָם מַה חוֹבָתוֹ בְּעוֹלָמוֹ,
וּלְמַה צָרִיךְ שֶׁיָּשִׂים מַבָּטוֹ וּמְגַמָּתוֹ בְּכָל אֲשֶׁר הוּא
עָמֵל כָּל יְמֵי חַיָּיו.

*The foundation of serving Hashem is that a
person should understand clearly why he was
created, and what his goals in life are.*

Mesillas Yesharim, Chapter 1 (Paraphrased)

Imagine, early one morning, you are walking past a block-long construction site. You see large cranes, heavy earth-moving machines, and bulldozers all gathered around. The workmen in hardhats are milling about in anxious anticipation. This is a major project, it is the first day of actual work, and it is almost time to break ground. Suddenly, a loud siren pierces the air and the site foreman signals all the workers to an emergency meeting.

"This is one of the biggest projects ever undertaken in the history of the city," he announces over the megaphone. "The plans call for 110 floors, poured concrete over steel girders. It is to be one of the largest, yet safest buildings ever built. But it seems there's been a mistake in calculations — we are over budget. In fact, we're so over-extended that the only way we can continue this project is if we change the plans. Normally for this type of structure, we would dig down hundreds of feet into the bedrock to secure a solid foundation, but the cost of doing that is prohibitive. So we've decided to just begin the building from the ground floor up. We will eliminate the foundation. We begin construction in ten minutes." And, with that, he ends the meeting.

Every worker there would look on in shock, thinking, "How can you build a building without a foundation?" It will never stand. No matter how solid the materials, no matter how well-planned the building, if the very foundation upon which it stands is lacking, one strong wind will topple the entire structure.

▼

The Basis of Our Religion

The *Mesillas Yesharim* tells us that the very foundation of our religion, the bedrock upon which it rests, is one core question: *Why did Hashem create me? What am I doing here? What is the purpose of my life?*

But this isn't simply an important issue — one of those interesting, theoretical questions worth pondering — it is the basis for everything we do, the foundation of everything we're living for. If a person doesn't ask and answer this question, then the rest of his life is built upon quicksand.

Oddly enough, if you were to conduct a survey of educated Jews and ask them why Hashem created man, you would likely get a number of answers:

"To serve Hashem."

"To do mitzvos."

"To learn."

"To make the world a better place."

"I'm not sure."

While they all may be very worthwhile and fine concepts, the *Mesillas Yesharim* is teaching us that they're *not* the reason that Hashem put us on the planet, and certainly not the basis for everything that we do.

It is intriguing that many people can't correctly answer this question. It is, however, even more compelling that most people don't even ask it. You might wonder: is it possible that thinking, intelligent people don't feel an overwhelming need to answer this question? How can a person live without knowing *why*? How can you make life decisions without an answer? How can you plan a family without a clear understanding of the purpose of it all?

The ironic part is that this question isn't confined to religion. It is a universal question that every human being must address. If I accept that God created this world and all that it contains, that means that God created me as well. Then the question is: why? What am I doing here? What is expected of me? Why was I created?

The answer to this question will impact on every decision I will ever make. It will set my priorities, and determine my lifestyle. It will define my values and calibrate how I measure success. More than anything, it will establish my goals and aspirations in life.

Is it possible that a person can go about this thing called life without having worked out a solid answer to this question? Isn't the answer going to profoundly affect his life more than anything else imaginable?

An Apparition

As an illustration, imagine it is a quiet summer evening.

You are walking along the beach, looking out at the calmness of the ocean when you notice what looks like a faint light far off on the horizon. Slowly, the light seems to grow larger and brighter, then brighter still, until it lights up the entire ocean. Suddenly, a towering figure appears. It looks like the form of a man in long robes. You can't make out any features, but it is huge and shining with a white glow. Then, without warning, a powerful voice booms out over the horizon:

"MOISHE!"

"Yee-eesss???" you meekly respond.

"I have been sent to tell you the secret of Creation…"

"Oh, my goodness! A *malach*. An angel is speaking to me! Yes. Yes. Please tell me. What is the secret of Creation?"

"The secret to understanding all of life is to understand why Hashem created the world."

"Yes, yes. Tell me. I'm ready. What is it? What is the reason behind it all?"

"The reason that Hashem created the world, and all that it contains, is so that you should make money."

"So… that I should make money?"

"Yes. So that you should make money."

"Money? I mean, that's it? That's the reason for everything? That's the reason that Hashem made the heavens and the earth, the oceans and the rivers?"

"Yes, so that you should make money. And lots of it. Hashem doesn't want you to just earn a living. Hashem wants you to earn as much money as you possibly can. He wants you to work from morning to night, long after you have earned more money than you, your children, and your children's children can possibly spend. Hashem wants you to work as hard as you can to earn even more money than that. That is the great secret of Creation."

And with those words, the angel leaves.

Wouldn't you imagine that such a conversation would

have a great effect on your future? Wouldn't you imagine that it would influence your choice in schooling, in jobs, and in how you spend your time? It should determine every aspect of your life.

While it is unlikely that you will ever have a *malach* speak directly to you, and it is even less likely that *that* will be the message he will deliver to you, this question is the single greatest defining criterion that will shape your life. *Why did Hashem create me? What am I doing here? What is my purpose in Creation?*

Living without Direction

Yet one of the curious facts about the human race is that we don't deal with this question. It is ignored, glossed over, just sort of skipped in the busyness that we call living. How is it possible that every human being hasn't grappled with this question and come to a firm answer to it? How is it possible that the vast majority of the human race is satisfied with saying inane things like, "I guess there are some questions that we can never know the answer to," or "One day, I will find an answer to the really big deal questions in life."

How do you make decisions without an answer? How do you chart a life without an answer? How do you *live* without an answer?

Interestingly, in every area other than life itself, we think things out, preparing ahead of time, anticipating all eventualities. What neighborhood will I live in? What type of school do I want my children to go to? What type of friends would I like to keep? We plan everything from next year's vacation to our retirement, but the single greatest question behind it all somehow eludes our focus.

When asked, "How do you intend to earn a living?" very few people respond, "Oh, I'm sure that something will just sort of come my way." When a person is sick, he doesn't just sort of wander around the block and hope to end up at the doctor's office.

It seems that in every other aspect of life, we have everything so worked out, but when it comes to the single biggest issue of our entire lives, we leave it up to, "Well, I guess eventually I'll figure out the answer."

Can I Borrow the Car?

We wouldn't allow our children to run about without direction. Imagine that your eighteen-year-old son says to you, "My friend is getting married in California and I'd like to go to the wedding. Do you mind if I borrow your car?"

You are hesitant about the idea, so you ask him, "How long do you think it will take? Do you have directions? Have you planned where you will be sleeping? Do you have enough money for gas and food?"

"Well... I haven't really thought about all those things," he responds. "I just thought I'd get in the car, start driving, and kind of like figure it out along the way."

I doubt you would find his answer very satisfactory. Yet that is the way we live. Without a plan, without direction, just sort of hoping against hope that we get it right.

The saddest part of it is that if you don't look for an answer, it is unlikely that you will ever find one. You will go about life, bobbing from shore to shore without an anchor, never quite understanding why things don't make sense, never quite living life to its fullest because your focus is constantly changing. You'll never accomplish your purpose in life. (And even if you did, you sure wouldn't know it.) How gratifying can such a life be? How much life satisfaction can you expect, living that way?

This seems to be a quirk in human nature. We can be so focused on *what* we are doing yet never address the question of *why* we are doing it. We get so caught up in getting things done that we don't focus on whether they were worth getting done in the first place.

THINK

Tom Watson, founder of IBM, built his company upon core principles of excellence. His vision was to create a truly great company. His management team was made up of some of the most experienced, talented business leaders of his time. Yet as you walked into his office, there was an arch over his desk with the word "THINK" etched into it. He found that even captains of industry, leaders in the world of commerce, tended to go to sleep at the switch, getting so caught up in the trees that they couldn't see the forest. The one message that he wanted to convey to his people was: THINK.

As ironic as it sounds, we tend not to think. A man can be brilliant, scholarly and erudite, but if his brain isn't on, it's worthless. To be successful in life, the one question that a person must THINK about is: *Why am I here? What is life about?*

Asking this question can bring about the single greatest change in your life, and not dealing with it can mean living a life without direction.

A Yellow Belt in Five Styles

Probably the greatest cost to a person living life without a clear purpose is that he won't reach a fraction of his potential. He will become like the young man who was a yellow belt in five styles of karate.

When this fellow was in grade school, he was fascinated with the martial arts, so he convinced his parents to let him study karate. He enrolled in a school and learned the stances, the kicks, and the punches. He was a diligent student, and after about a year of training, he was ready for his yellow belt test, the first rank. He took the test and passed.

Shortly after that, his family moved to another city, but the only karate school he could find there practiced a different style of karate. So he began again from the basics, with new stances, new kicks, and new punches. Again he progressed well, and again he took his yellow belt test — now in the new style — and passed.

Soon the time came for him to go away to high school. In that city, he again searched for a karate school, and the only one he could find taught a third style of karate. So he had to start from the basics with the new stances, new kicks, and new punches. And in this style as well, he was awarded a yellow belt. Midpoint through high school, he switched yeshivahs, and began the same process again.

At the end of five years of disciplined training, this young man had attained the rank of yellow belt in five styles — a beginner! Had he spent the same amount of time and effort in one style, he would have attained the rank of black belt — a master. The ironic part was that he applied himself and worked hard, but because his focus kept changing and he had to start from the beginning over and over again, his advancement was stymied. At the end, he remained a rank beginner.

Changing Currency

This story has a message. Most people spend their lives with changing priorities. That which is important at one stage becomes insignificant at another. To a young boy growing up in America, *sports* are king. That is what really counts in his world. But that doesn't last; it is soon replaced by *friends* and *being popular*. As he matures, *grades* and *what college he gets into* become the measure of success. Within a short while, his *career* and *making money* are all that really matter. Yet this also passes, and shortly, he will trade away huge amounts of his wealth to build his *reputation*. As he nears retirement, his *health* and his *future nursing home* become his primary concern.

Throughout life, whatever is precious and coveted at one stage becomes devalued and traded away when new priorities take over. The currency is constantly changing. The result of this is that while someone may do well at each stage in life, the totality of what he accomplished may not amount to much. He became a *yellow belt* in five styles.

On the Deathbed

One of the costs of not asking the fundamental questions

of life is that people end up in some rather sad situations. Often, at the end of a person's life — when it is too late to do anything about it — he has bitter regrets about the way he spent his time.

Many people have strong misgivings on their deathbed. But very few of those regrets are for not spending more time in the office. "Gee, I really wish that I had worked eighty hours a week, instead of the seventy I had been putting in for thirty years." "I deeply regret taking off Sundays to spend with my family."

The vast majority of the world leaves this earth with unfulfilled dreams. The tragic part is that for many people those dreams were within easy grasp — they just didn't focus on them. Because they had the wrong priorities, they shaped their vision and currency on what was important at the time. That currency changed as they got older and wiser — but then it was too late.

There is a story told about a CEO of a major corporation who was retiring. In honor of the event, the company threw a gala dinner. It was a black tie affair with all of the officers, executives, and their spouses in attendance. The CEO got up to speak. He looked out over the audience and said, "I can tell that many of you would like my job. But if you want it, you have to be ready to pay the price. Let me tell you about my job. My daughter was recently married. At the wedding, I looked around and I realized that I didn't recognize any of her friends. I didn't know what books she read. I didn't know what she liked or didn't like. In short, I didn't know my daughter. If you want my job, you have to pay the price. *That* is the price. I don't think it is worth it."

And he sat down.

Those are very sad words. Not because a man made a mistake, but because he made it with such calculation and self-sacrifice. He wasn't basking in the sun. He was a powerful goal-setter — driven, ambitious, hard at work — but working hard toward the wrong goals. Racing down the highway of life — headed in the wrong direction.

The Saddest Words Ever Spoken

Among the saddest words that a human can ever utter are: *could've, would've, should've.* I *could've* accomplished a lot more. I *would've* made better choices. I *should've* lived my life differently.

This is a sobering concept. What if you lived your entire life for the wrong purpose and with the wrong goals in mind? It's not pleasant to wake up at eighty years of age and say, *"According to what you've just said, I wasted my entire life."*

Even worse, what if those were conscious lifestyle choices that came at a great expense? What happens when a person sacrifices all that he has — his time and his family — only to find out later that the cause itself was false?

One of the realities of life is that you will work hard. No matter what you do, no matter how you live, from the day you arrive on this planet until the day that you leave, you will be very actively engaged in this thing we call living — working, planning, doing. The only question is: are the goals that you are working toward worth achieving?

Where Are You Headed?

The *Mesillas Yesharim* teaches us that the first principle

of leading a successful life is knowing what you want out of it. Know where you are headed. Know your currency, know your value system, and then set goals in accordance with it.

But therein lies the problem. How does a young person know where life will bring him when he is older? Which human is wise enough to know where he will be in twenty years? How can anyone know what he will consider important and valuable when he is in a different stage of life?

When you ask a five-year-old, "What do you want to be when you grow up?" he might tell you he wants to be a fireman, a policeman, or a basketball player. In reality, he isn't telling you what he wants to be when he grows up. He is telling you what he wants to be *now*, if he were grown up.

He is telling you, based on his five-year-old understanding of life, what he values and considers important. He can't tell what he will value when he is older. He has no way of knowing what he will consider important and significant then. He is telling what he wants to be now. And according to his current understanding of the world, he would like to be Superman, Batman or a UPS driver.

In this sense, one of the most difficult things for any human to do is to set a life course that will make him happy thirty years in the future. How can anyone possibly know what will be important to him then? How can we know what we will consider successful then?

The Plan

The *Mesillas Yesharim* tells us that Hashem didn't just create man and leave him to figure it all out. Hashem didn't design an entire world for man, put him into it with a mission, and then stand aside saying, "But I am not going to tell you what it is. It's a secret. Go figure it out."

Hashem gave us a clear, definitive blueprint, an exact guidebook with clear directions on how to live our lives and the underlying reasons for it. The key to true success is to open that book, learn its words of truth, and mold our lives accordingly.

May this chapter be a zechus for the hatzlachah of our family.
Moishe and Chavy Vegh

CHAPTER 3

Immutable Laws Of Nature

ספר שמות פרק כ

(ו) ועשה חסד לאלפים לאהבי ולשמרי מצותי.

(רש״י) **ועושה חסד** - שאדם עושה לשלם שכר עד לאלפים דור
נמלאת מדה טובה יתירה על מדת פורעניות אחת על חמש
מאות שזו לארבעה דורות וזו לאלפים. (סוטה יא)

*He does kindness for two thousand genera-
tions, to those who He loves, and those who
guard His mitzvos.*

*{Rashi} If a man acts righteously he is paid
back for two thousand generations. The good
therefore outweighs the bad by a ratio of 500:1.
When it comes to paying back evil, Hashem
only pays back for four generations, yet when it
comes to paying back good deeds, Hashem pays
back for two thousand generations.*

*"He does kindness for thousands of generations, to those who
He loves and those who guard His mitzvos." – Shemos* 20:6

Hashem formed this world with immutable laws of nature.
Heat tends to rise. Gases tend to expand. Heavy objects tend
to fall. These tenets guide all of physicality throughout the
unimaginably vast cosmos. The same molecular structure,
laws, and patterns that govern matter on earth apply in the
most distant galaxy — all in perfect order, all in equilibrium
and balance. As with the physical world, so, too, the spiritual
world. All of Creation conforms to absolute laws that Hashem
set into motion and continues to use in guiding it.

Rashi explains that when the Torah says that Hashem
pays back the wicked for four generations and the righteous
for two thousand generations, this teaches us one of the op-

erating principles of Creation: the measure of good versus bad in the world.

The ratio of two thousand generations to four is 500:1. This is the proportion of *good* to *bad*, the balance of reward to punishment, of pleasure to pain. In other words, for any displeasure in existence, there is five hundred times the enjoyment. For any suffering, there is five hundred times the joy. Before Hashem formed the world, He set this ratio as one of its guiding doctrines. This, however, requires understanding.

Life Is Great!

Imagine that you met a man and politely asked him, "How's life?" to which he responded, "Life? Life is great! Not just great, but FANTASTIC! Only goodness and blessing. From the moment I open my eyes in the morning until I close them at night, all that I experience is unbridled bliss, joy and contentment. Pleasures upon pleasures. Delight upon delight. Nothing but unending satisfaction. Life is awesome!!!"

While his description may intrigue you, in your mind, you would probably think, "What planet does *he* come from?!" Granted life is good — it certainly has its moments. But what human being would describe his life as unending ecstasy?

Yet that is what Rashi seems to be saying. A ratio of 500:1 means that the rough spots in life are so overshadowed by the enormity of good that they are almost nonexistent. For every headache I endure, I enjoy five hundred times the pleasure. For every stomach cramp I suffer with, I benefit from five hundred measures of delight. Can anyone say that their "pleasures" outweigh their "pains" five hundred to one? How do we reconcile this principle with the reality of our lives?

CHAPTER 4

Appreciating This World

Imagine a man who, at age thirty-five, becomes blind. Being a fighter, he struggles for ten years to create a productive life for himself and succeeds — to a degree. One day, his doctor informs him of an experimental procedure that, if successful, would enable him to see again. He is both frightened and exuberant. If it works, he regains his sight. If it fails, he might die.

He gathers his family to discuss his options, and after much debate he announces, "I am going ahead with it." The operation is scheduled, and the long awaited day arrives. Paralyzed with dread, he is wheeled into the operating room. Given sedatives, he sleeps through the entire ten-hour operation.

When he wakes up, his first thought is to open his eyes. He prepares himself for the moment. He will now find out how he will spend the rest of his life. He gets ready, musters up his courage, and flexes his eyelids. They don't move! In a panic he cries out, "NURSE!"

The nurse calmly explains that his bandages won't come off for at least three more days. So he waits. Each moment like a decade, each hour a lifetime. Finally it is time. With his family gathered around, with the doctors and nurses at his side, the surgeon begins removing the gauze. The first bandage is off, now the second. The surgeon says, "Open your eyes." He does. And he sees!

For the first time in ten years, he looks out and experiences the sights of this world — and he is struck by it all. Struck by the brilliance of colors and shapes. Moved by the beauty and magnificence of all that is in front of him. He looks out the window and sees a meadow covered with beautiful, green grass. He sees flowers in full bloom. He looks up and sees a clear, blue sky. He sees people — the faces of loved ones that have been only images in his mind, the sight of his own children that he hasn't seen in ten years. Tears well up in his eyes as he says, "Doctor, what can I ever do to repay you for what you have given me? This magnificent gift of sight! Thank you!"

Appreciating Our Gifts

We are that man. Each morning we open our eyes and we see. Every day we enjoy the remarkable gift of vision. And, we can experience the same feeling of elation that he felt on a daily basis... if we train ourselves to feel it. Sight is a precious, unparalleled gift that we are supposed to stop and think about. Not once in a lifetime. Not even once a year. Every day.

Part of our spiritual growth is learning to appreciate the gifts that we have. One of the blessings we say each morning thanks Hashem for this most wonderful gift of sight. It was designed to be said with an outpouring of emotion.

We humans are a curious breed. We can have treasures for years without ever thinking of them, not once stopping to appreciate the wealth we have been given... until something happens. Then it is, "*Hashem, why me? Of all the people on the planet, why did You pick me?*" Till then there wasn't a moment of reflection. Not one thank-you. Not even a recognition of it being a gift. But once it is gone, the complaints find their home.

Unfortunately, we don't take the time to think about the many gifts that we have. We become so accustomed to them that we almost don't know they exist. How many times do we stop and appreciate that we have legs, arms and hands? How many mornings do we wake up and just take the time to recognize that we have our health and well-being? How much richer is our life because we have eyes with which to see, fingers with which to feel, ears with which to hear, a tongue with which to taste, and a nose with which to smell?

Each of these senses was created by Hashem with wisdom and forethought so that we should live fuller, richer, and more complete lives. There is so much about this world that was custom-designed for our enjoyment. But it takes focus and training to gain an appreciation for the riches that we possess.

Revisiting Creation

To help do just that, let's take a step back from life as

we know it and imagine the very moment when Hashem created the world.

Picture if you will vast emptiness. Nothing. Absolute absence of anything.

I remember when my daughter was six years old and we were discussing Bereishis (Creation), there was one issue that she couldn't come to terms with.

"Abba," she said to me. "I understand that before Hashem created the world there was nothing, not even light and dark, but what color was it?"

The difficulty she was having was that we are so used to the world as it is that the concept of *before Creation* is difficult for us to fathom. The idea of the absence of anything — before there was a world, before there was even matter, space, or any substance to hold it in — is very difficult for us corporeal beings to comprehend. We keep falling back to our way of viewing things in a physical setting, and absolute void has no place in our world.

But let's try for a moment to envision a vast empty nothingness. There is no space, no matter. There isn't even time because time only exists in a physical world. And Creation begins. Out of nothing — because there is nothing. From nowhere — because there is no place. At this absolute first moment in time, Hashem brings forth matter, the very building blocks of Creation. Then come darkness and light, not even separated, but intermingled — a patch of light here, a flash of darkness there. Next come the heavens and the earth, then the planets and the stars, the fish in the sea, the birds in the sky, and all of the animals of the earth. And on the final day, at almost the last moment of Creation, comes man.

Every part of Creation had to be thought out. There were no givens. There was no imitating or accepting the status quo because before Creation, there was nothing to imitate or use as a model. Every part and every element of this world had to be planned and designed from scratch. When we take this huge leap of understanding, we will see the abundance of goodness that Hashem has bestowed upon the world.

Color

Let's start with something basic — color. The world is fantastically rich in color, with so many gradations, shades, and hues.

Color is something that we take for granted. Of course, there is color in the world; it was always there. But Hashem created this thing that we call color, and He put it in the world for a particular reason: so that we should enjoy what we see. The world didn't have to be this way. If Hashem was only concerned with functionality — creating a world that could be used — black and white would have sufficed. We would still be able to recognize everything, even shadows and depth, within the spectrum of the gray scale. If you remember watching black and white TV, it did a fine job, but it lacked a dimension, and so it wasn't as enjoyable. Hashem wants us to enjoy this world, and so He created the entity called color.

Look out on a fall day and see the trees in their glory, the seemingly endless array of brilliant reds, oranges, and yellows forming a magnificent tapestry stretching across the mountains. Look out at the sun as it sets and see the full radiant spectrum of an artist's pallet, painted against a powdery gray backdrop.

If the world was created for practical reasons only, all of the beauty within it wouldn't have to exist. But Hashem put it all here — from magnificent floral scenes to exotic sea life, from the glory of the night sky to the clear aqua green of the ocean, from a flower in bloom to the plume of a jungle parrot, all of the pomp and ceremony of a sunrise — a world created in Technicolor. Why create it that way? Keep it plain and simple. Why go through all of the effort? The answer is for one reason: so that man should benefit. Hashem did all of this for us so that we should look out at the world and enjoy its beauty.

Taste, Texture and Aroma

Color is only *one* of the pleasures that we enjoy but take for granted. What about food? Food is something that we need to maintain our energy levels and health. If its only function were nutrition and nothing more, then all the foods that we eat should taste like soggy cardboard. Yet they don't. There are so many different types of foods, each with a unique flavor, texture, and aroma. Why create them that way? Why not make it all taste like oatmeal? Again, for one reason: so that man should enjoy. So that eating, which we have to do, shouldn't be a chore, but a pleasure. Taste is something that Hashem added solely for our benefit — for our delight.

An awful lot of thought went into creating the different foods that we eat. I once heard R' Avigdor Miller, *zt"l*, describe an orange. When you peel an orange, there are wedges inside. If you look closely, each one of these wedges is surrounded by a thin membrane. When you pull back the membrane and look inside, you will see many tiny sacs. Inside each of those sacs is the juice of the orange.

Why did Hashem create an orange in that manner, with thousands of little sacs? The reason is simple: to further enhance our enjoyment. Did you ever see one of those children's candies with a liquid center? They're advertised with the slogan, *"Bite in for a burst of flavor."* When you bite into an orange, you also get a burst of flavor. The juice of the orange is contained within those many small sacs, so when you bite into it, there is a release of juice in the form of a burst, and that adds to the enjoyment of eating the orange. Hashem created those sacs so that there would be another dimension to our enjoyment. The sensation of eating an orange would be different without them. Oranges would still taste delicious, but this is an additional aspect that Hashem wanted us to benefit from, so He designed an orange in this way.

Food Coloring

Do you ever wonder why apples are red on the outside?

It's for the same reason that laundry detergents come packaged in bright colors. Proctor and Gamble spent millions of dollars on research to determine which color has the greatest eye appeal. They have done countless studies proving that putting Tide in a neon orange container will result in more sales. Shoppers favor it, and they will reach for it before the other brands. Cheerios has been in that same yellow box for over sixty years now! Studies show that this particular shade of yellow sells more cereal than any other color. People simply prefer it.

So, too, Hashem made apples red because it is a nice color to look at, and that makes eating the apples more enjoyable. As any chef knows, the presentation adds to the dish. Hashem designed foods with eye appeal to enhance our experience of eating. Keep in mind: food is only needed to provide nourishment. Any other feature is there because Hashem had a specific reason for it. Many of these were created simply so that we should have greater pleasure and enjoyment.

Texture

Here is another example: what happens when you bite into an apple?

You don't get that burst of flavor that you get when you bite into an orange. You get a crunch. Why is that? Why not design all fruit the same?

The reason an apple is crunchy is that it is *fun* to crunch on food. That's why your supermarket has an entire aisle, seventy feet long, floor to ceiling, stocked with breakfast cereals, each one bragging to be crispier than the next. Crispy, crispier, crispiest. *"Ours is so crispy, we even include ear plugs for your neighbors down the block!"*

Why is each company trying to convince you that its cereal is the crispiest? Because it's *fun* to bite into something crunchy; we like that sensation. So General Mills makes their cereals crunchy, and when Hashem made apples, He designed their cells to form hard walls so that when we bite into them, we get a texture that provides a crunch. It didn't have to be that way. Hashem designed it so that we should enjoy it. (For the life of me I still can't figure out why bananas are mushy! But I guess that sometimes we are in the mood for a texture that is soft and squishy.)

A typical salad contains many different vegetables: tomatoes, cucumbers, green peppers, lettuce, and mushrooms. Each one is distinct with its own shape, texture, and flavor; each contributes its unique qualities to the whole. Why create them that way? Why not make them all brown like beans? Why don't they all taste like potatoes? The reason is that it wouldn't have been much fun. The food we eat comes in so many assorted flavors and textures, each one appealing to a different element of our tastes so that we should enjoy them. Hashem invested a remarkable amount of detail and concern for us to have pleasure.

Aroma

What about aroma?

Did you ever go to a restaurant when you had a cold? The waiter brought out your favorite dish, and your mouth was watering at the sight of it, but when you began eating it, somehow it didn't taste right. You just couldn't enjoy it. Scientists now recognize that most of our sense of taste comes through smells. When Hashem created food, He added this dimension of wonderful aromas to enhance our taste experience. Not only do our foods have different tastes and textures, they all have distinct smells — to contribute to our enjoyment.

But, there's more. Did you ever notice that when you peel an orange, a fine mist of juice sprays up? If you pay careful attention, you will see that the outer skin has tiny bubbles in it. When the skin is broken, the liquid inside is released in a fine mist that carries the aroma of the orange. Why did Hashem go through all of the effort to design those tiny bubbles of juice in the skin? For one reason: so that when you peel an orange, you will smell the fragrance and hunger for it. When you hunger for a food, your enjoyment of it is greater.

It wasn't enough that the flavor of the orange is a distinctive mix of sweetness and tang, and that the wedges were made up of little sacs to provide that *"burst of flavor."* Maybe we wouldn't be quite hungry enough, so Hashem designed the tiny bubbles in the skin to increase our enjoyment.

It didn't have to be that way. To get our daily dosage of Vitamin C, we could have done just as well without all of these enhancements. But Hashem wanted to add pleasure to our eating.

The Ratio of 500:1

This seems to be the answer to Rashi. The 500:1 ratio is accurate. Not only did Hashem design a world with countless features fashioned for our enjoyment, He gave us five senses carefully constructed to allow us to discern the most delicate differences.

The *eye* is brilliantly designed to deliver images with vivid, gripping clarity, and the brain is fashioned to interpret these messages, so that we experience an explosion of sight — in thousands upon thousands of gradient colors in different hues, intensities and vibrancies. The *ear* is finely tuned to convey all of the nuances of sound from the haunting tone of the flute to the crashing roar of the percussions. And thousands and thousands of variant sounds that combine to form unified, pleasing melodies to enhance our experience of hearing. The *tongue, mouth* and *palette* are so wondrously designed to be able to discern between tastes: sweet and sour, salty and bitter in immeasurable combinations.

It didn't have to be that way. All of the enhancements and extras were put there for our pleasure.

Did Hashem Succeed?

Focusing on this gives us a hint to the giving, loving kindliness of Hashem. And it shows us how much He wants us to enjoy this world. However, it also brings us to a critical question: do people notice these things? All of these features were designed with us in mind. Do we benefit from them?

It seems that for most people the answer is no, the world doesn't bring them much enjoyment at all. And this is a rather curious fact. Hashem invested incredible care to bring forth everything that we need to enjoy life — and most people don't even notice it, let alone appreciate it. But why? Why don't we benefit from all of these pleasures?

Even more perplexing is that Hashem is very capable. We see from the vastness, complexity and intricate wonder of Creation that Hashem is very effective at doing that which He does. It is clear that Hashem wants man to enjoy this world. The ratio of pleasure to pain really is five hundred to one. Yet when it comes to man actually having pleasure — if it could be — it seems that Hashem failed. How is that possible? What does it mean?

The solution to this dilemma isn't simply for us to learn to "appreciate what we have." Rather, it underscores a basic element of the human personality and requires a fundamental understanding of man. However, before we deal with this dilemma, we need to take another step back and recognize something unique about our generation.

This chapter is sponsored by
Kenneth and Julie Pinczower

CHAPTER 5

More Money Equals More Happiness

My grandmother grew up in Poland before the First World War. Her family was considered well off; they lived in a two-room house. That meant two rooms. One for the parents, and one where the kids slept, ate, played, did chores, cooked, bathed, and cleaned their clothes. That was it. Two rooms, period. And believe me, the rooms weren't large, and the families weren't small.

Today, when we go on vacation and "*rough it*" by putting the whole family — parents and two kids — in one motel room, it's cute and cozy... for an evening. But that was the amount of space people lived in with all of their belongings, all of the time. That was home. On floors made of dirt, with furniture consisting of the barest table and a few chairs, with wood-burning fireplaces that had to be stocked by chopping trees — they lived. Their walls were filled with cracks that let in the cold air of winter, but held in the sweltering heat of summer. They drove horses to the market and bathed only on special occasions — without phones, without TV, without running water or electricity, people lived. Regular people. Our people. Our grandparents and great-grandparents lived.

We aren't any different than they were. They walked, ate, slept, and breathed as we do. They weren't born on a different planet, and they didn't live a thousand years ago. Yet their lives were so different from ours that it is difficult for us to even imagine ourselves in that setting.

Luxuries of Yesteryear

My great aunt, Tante Perel, came over from Poland before my grandmother. When my grandmother arrived in America and visited Tante Perel for the first time, Tante Perel told her in an excited voice, "You must see this! You won't believe your eyes! Our building has a bathroom in the apartment itself!" It was a standard of luxury beyond what they could have imagined.

While it may sound like ancient history to us, it wasn't that long ago that people used outhouses. In the freezing cold of winter, they would don a coat and go out to the back where they found a bare hut. In that world, there were no such things as cars and planes and buses. There were no paved roads and highways. If you had somewhere to go, you got into a horse-drawn wagon and bumped along a stone path for hours until your insides wanted to come out.

Heat was a thing for the rich. My father had a friend who went to yeshivah in a remote part of Eastern Europe. This man had a handy way of telling whether it was a cold morning. He would leave a vessel filled with water next to his bed each night so that he could wash as soon as he woke up in the morning. Before washing, he would look into the vessel. If it had iced over, he knew it was a cold day!

I want to remind you that water doesn't turn to ice at 58 degrees. And not at 48 either. He slept in the very room that the water froze in! These days, we set our thermostats to a comfy 72, and if it goes below 62, someone will complain, "Hey, it's freezing in here!" If your furnace goes out, you immediately call the heating company — it's an emergency! And if they say, "We'll have a technician come out to look at it in the morning," you'll go to a friend's house for the night. "It's 50 degrees in my house! How can anyone survive in that kind of cold!?" Yet people did survive — people who were no different than you or me, and at temperatures well below 50 degrees.

We Are So Wealthy

The comforts and material possessions that we take for granted today were unimaginable a few generations ago. If you walk down an aisle in Wal-Mart, everything you see is available to be had — in whatever color, shape and texture you like. And for the most part, we have the money to buy it.

To give you an illustration, I once gave a talk on this topic, and after the lecture, a woman came over to tell me a story. She was friendly with a new immigrant, a Russian woman. She took her adopted friend on their first outing to a large supermarket. When the Russian woman walked into the produce section and saw the abundance and plenty on display, she was so overcome with emotion that she fainted.

In all of her years, she had never seen so much food so readily available. During the Communist regime, it was considered a regular part of the day to wait for hours on food lines. Nowadays, if we are held up for ten minutes at the checkout counter, we are already looking for a new supermarket.

Here is another example. If you own a house built before World War II, you will probably notice that no matter how large it is, there never seems to be enough closet space. The home might have sizable rooms, plenty of bedrooms and lots of living space, but tiny, undersized closets. Why is that? Why didn't they build closets to match the size of the house?

It's because the house was built for people living in those times. No one then would dream that we would own the amount of clothing that we do now. I spoke to a woman who grew up in the 1930's, and she told me she had two dresses: one for weekdays and one for Shabbos. She wasn't poor; she came from a typical home. That was considered normal. So they built homes back then with closets that were ample for the wardrobes of those times.

▼

Our Clothing

Now we have racks and racks of clothing: suits, shirts, slacks, sweaters, winter coats, summer jackets, light fall coats, ties, belts, pocketbooks, and matching accessories, not to mention shoes. My *rebbe*, R' A. H. Leibowitz, *zt"l*, grew up in America in the 1920's. When he was a young boy, he wore a hole in the bottom of the one pair of shoes he owned. He didn't have the heart to ask his father for the twenty-five cents that it would cost to have new soles put on. So he figured out his own solution. He put a piece of cardboard inside the shoe so that his socks wouldn't rub out on the concrete when he walked. It worked well until the first rainy day. He walked outside and right into a puddle — splash! His new soles were gone.

Do we know anyone today who doesn't own a number of pairs of shoes? In black, blue, and brown — some for casual wear, others for dress. Gotta have at least one pair for running, another for basketball, and still others for bowling. Do you play golf? Of course, only an entirely separate wardrobe is fitting. And Heaven forefend to play tennis in basketball shoes!

Compared to Other Times

If we were to describe our wealth to people of a different generation, I don't think they would believe us. Kings in prior times didn't enjoy the luxuries that we do. If you look at portraits of King George, monarch of England before the Revolutionary War, you'll see him sitting on his throne in the comfort of his palace wearing layer upon layer of robes, topped off by a fur covering. Did you ever wonder why he was wearing all of those layers? The reason is that it was mighty cold in the king's palace! The King of England with all of his wealth had to stay warm by huddling up to a smoky fireplace that heated up only the part of his body that was facing it, not the rest of him that was facing the other way. His Highness had to walk through dimly lit, dank hallways at night. He had to sleep on a mattress of stuffed feathers. (Keep in mind, there were no chiropractors around to care for his aching back as he sunk down into thirty-six inches of duck feathers.) And when his brother, the Duke, was getting married, traveling to the wedding meant enduring a backbreaking carriage ride for the better part of a week. The crown jewels couldn't buy him the luxuries that we take for granted today.

The reality is that we are wealthy beyond belief. We enjoy comforts and abundance that are historically unprecedented. And it's not just the extremely affluent. The average tax-paying citizen of today lives in opulence and splendor that previous generations couldn't dream about.

And this is before we discuss the advances of technology that we enjoy. A friend of mine was flying into NYC, and after touching down, the plane stopped at a distance from the terminal. The flight attendant announced that there would be a slight delay as they waited for the walkway to be brought over. The passengers watched as a technician maneuvered a mobile gangplank into place. The person sitting next to my friend remarked, "Look at the wonders of technology. They even have moving walkways!"

My friend was flabbergasted. They had just been traveling five hundred miles an hour at an altitude of 32,000 feet. No cables, no wires — flying in the air. And this person was astonished by a mobile gangplank! What happened to amazement that man has so mastered the laws of gravity that he can fly? What happened to the astonishment of travelling across the world? That's yesterday's news. We are used to that. And so we take it for granted. But in reality the luxuries that we enjoy due to technological advances are fantastic: from iPods to e-mail, from packaged goods to microwaves, from laptop computers to a GPS.

------▼------

We Have Arrived —Are We Happy?

In short, we are wealthy beyond belief. We have riches that far, far exceed our needs. As a society, as a nation, and as individuals, we enjoy prosperity and abundance. We benefit from creature comforts that were unthinkable a generation ago. Everything is so readily available, so accessible, so easy. And so I have one question: now that we have so much, are we happy?

For centuries, all that man desired was freedom from tyranny and a homeland where he could enjoy liberty and safety. Armies went to war for it, entire generations sacrificed all that they had for it, and we now have it. We are there. We have finally arrived. Living in a free society with almost unlimited opportunity, we are easily able to find sustenance and enjoy unheard of wealth; we have it all. But are we happy? Now that we are there, is it all that we thought it was? Is this the dream that we were seeking? Are we any happier today than our ancestors in previous generations?

While it is difficult to compare such an abstract concept as *levels of happiness* between the generations, Richard Earlstein, an economic historian with the University of Southern California, did an eye-opening study. He compared the relationship of increasing income to happiness. He found that although the gross domestic product per capita in the US has more than doubled in the past half century, there has been absolutely no improvement in the percentage of happy people. We have more than twice the amount of goods available to each consumer, as compared to fifty years ago — twice as many cars, twice as many refrigerators, twice as many homes — yet we aren't any happier. He goes on to say, "Even though each generation has more than its predecessor, each generation wants more." He points out that one of the most enduring cultural beliefs is that a twenty percent increase in our income would make us perfectly happy, but it just isn't true. No sooner do we get that twenty percent increase then we need more, and we enter into an unending cycle.

Money Will Make Me Happy

This brings us to an odd phenomenon. It seems that there is an inherent cultural belief that money will solve all problems. *"If only I were a millionaire. Wow, life would be great! All of my troubles would be solved. I would be so happy."*

Even intelligent, thinking people get caught up in this myth, ceaselessly pursuing wealth, all the while thinking, at least in the back of their minds, that more money means more happiness. But it doesn't work, because no sooner do they get more, then they need even more than that.

This point is illustrated by a study of major lottery winners. These were people who won significant fortunes. Yet within one year of winning the jackpot, eighty percent were back at work. Eighty percent! That means all of those people who for years were saying, "Just wait till I win the jackpot. Just one big one and I'm gone! You won't see my face in this joint again." But within a year they are back, often at the same job they left. It is especially intriguing because many of the winners weren't in high-satisfaction employment. Often they were typical working class people who drove cabs, waited on tables, or worked in factories.

Bob the UPS Driver Wins Big

To put this into perspective, let's imagine Bob, the UPS driver. He hates his job, talks about quitting all the time. His favorite expression is, "A bad day at fishing is better than a good day at work."

Each week Bob sets out with a dollar and a dream to buy himself a lottery ticket, and waits for his numbers to come in. Then one day, lo and behold, Bob wins! And he wins big. Enough money that he doesn't have to work a day in his life again.

What happens?

First, Bob buys himself that ultimate fishing boat. Then he buys every imaginable lure and casting system known to man. Then off on a world cruise — to see the sights. Life could not be better. Day after carefree day...

From Morocco to Tunisia to Egypt, he covers the sun-scorched deserts on camelback. Then, dodging donkeys and goats, he makes his way through the dusty streets of Istanbul to see the dazzling bazaars. A quick stop over at the Turkish baths, then on to the Caribbean: Barbados, Curacao, then off to Costa Rica...

But then a funny thing happens. Bob gets bored. Been there. Done that. Kayaked the Amazon river, ATV'ed up the pyramids. Now what? Back to work he marches. Back to the same brown truck, back to the same brown pants and socks, back to the very same route. There's Bob picking up packages and dropping them off.

What Went Wrong?

What happened? What went wrong? All that he needed to truly enjoy life was some wealth — and he got it. What could be better? He so clearly knew that with just a little bit of money his life would be so totally and completely different. Yet, now he has it, and his life hasn't magically changed. He didn't suddenly find the potion of unending joy and eternal bliss.

The compelling part is that it's hard to find any real correlation between more money and greater happiness. And while we all *sort of* know that, we live our lives as if it weren't true. We have been socialized into this mindless acceptance of "more money equals more happiness." But it never works. The money looks so tempting, so alluring. It seems that it will fill all of our needs and wants. But at the end of the day, it leaves us just as thirsty — not for more money or more luxuries — but for something else. We just aren't satisfied.

Each person feels, "I'll be different. Just give me a couple of billion and I will be soooo happy." But he, too, gets the money, and life doesn't change — he's the same as he was before. The question is: why? Why doesn't it make him happy? It was all he ever wanted. It's all that he ever dreamed about. Now that he has it, why can't he just be happy?

What Is Missing?

This question is compounded because Hashem created a custom-made world with much thought and focus for our enjoyment. All of the beauty of Creation: from the brilliance of a sunset to the lushness of a tropical garden, all of the colors and hues fashioned so that we should benefit. All of the smells that we experience — from the gentle fragrance of a rose to the aroma of roast beef — were crafted for our benefit. All of the different colors, textures, and flavors of food formed for us to enjoy. Yet we don't enjoy them. Why not? For Heaven's sake, what is missing?

CHAPTER 6

The Pursuit Of Pleasure

"Whoever said money can't buy happiness isn't spending it right."
                                                                    — Lexus ad

Imagine that you find yourself shipwrecked on a deserted island. You haven't seen a soul in three days... or a piece of bread either for that matter. You are famished. Hungrier than you've ever been in your life, your every thought is on just finding something to eat. Anything, anything, to take away that emptiness inside your stomach. Suddenly, you spot a crumpled paper bag, sitting in the shade of a palm tree. You open it. Inside is a dry, crusty, six-month-old peanut butter sandwich.

You lace into this sandwich with such fervor that you feel almost as if you're standing outside of yourself watching as you wolf it down. After swallowing every last crumb, you sit back to rest, no longer quite as hungry as before.

The Difference between Pleasure and Passion

Let's analyze this situation. There is no question that you ate that sandwich with great hunger — you had *passion*. However, would you call this one of the most pleasurable activities of your life? Do you think that for the rest of your days, you would look back fondly on the feeling of the dry bread as it scratched your throat? Or the acrid taste of the spoiled peanut butter going down?

This is an example of doing something with great appetite, but not deriving much *pleasure*. *Pleasure* is the amount of enjoyment that you receive while doing an activity. *Passion* is the desire, the pull you have to that activity. That peanut butter sandwich was eaten with great passion, but it gave very little pleasure. While this difference may sound obvious, it isn't. And it is one of the keys to understanding what really drives us.

In our minds, we often mix the two concepts together as if to say, "If I have such a strong desire to do something, it must be because there is a lot of pleasure in it." But that isn't always the case.

Chemical/Alcohol Addiction

There are things that we desire that bring us little pleasure, and there are things that bring us great pleasure that we don't instinctively desire.

Ask an addict — whether to alcohol, chemicals or whatever — to describe how much *pleasure* he receives from drinking or from drugs. Most likely, he will tell you that the first experiences were great:

"I got high, wow!"

"There was nothing like it!"

But if you ask him now that he is hooked, now that he is a slave to the bottle or the pills, to describe the experience, it sounds much more out of Gehinnom (purgatory) than out of Heaven.

"Being chained to the bottle."

"Desperately needing to drink — no matter what the cost."

"Knowing that the next drink might kill me, yet not being able to stop myself."

While the addict may have started out motivated by the pleasure, the desire has become so powerful that it controls him, even when the activity no longer brings him pleasure. Not only aren't addicts motivated by pleasure, they often find no enjoyment in it anymore. It leaves them empty and depressed, down and out — but they need it all the same.

This distinction between pleasure and passion becomes critical in understanding what pleasure really is and why it seems so difficult for man to find enjoyment. But to understand man's relationship to pleasures, we need to take one more step in understanding the way that Hashem made him.

Hedonists Are Bound to Fail

Did you ever hear the expression, "The average man thinks he is smarter than the average man"? It seems to be a quirk of human nature that people feel the rules of human nature apply to everyone — except me. Me, I am just... different.

So let's assume that while I know that "there's more to life than money," that's true for all those little people who don't know how to spend their money. But me? I am way smarter than that. I know having money in the bank won't make me happy. It's knowing how to *spend it* that brings happiness. Just give me enough money, and I will be as happy as a lark.

Let's take this a step further. Imagine that I get a chance to try it out. My greatest wish is granted — I win the lotto. But not just *a* lotto, I win the largest single payout in history of the US lottery: 365 million dollars in cash. Awesome joy! I made it. I have arrived. I am rich! Rich! RICH!

And so, since all that has been standing between me and some real happiness has been this lack of money thing, now that I have it, I intend to enjoy it! So I set out to have pleasure. But not a little bit of pleasure. Not some haphazard come-as-it-may pleasure, but real pleasure, heaps and heaps of it. Pleasures upon pleasures. As much downright pure pleasure as I can possibly cram in. *Eat, drink and be merry for tomorrow we may die! Let's party!*

My Life of Pleasure

The first thing I do is buy myself a private island in the Pacific. What better place to enjoy life than there? I hire a team of butlers and maids and an entire dining room staff. An Italian chef for breakfast, Mediterranean cuisine for lunch, and for dinner nothing but the finest: my personal French chef.

And so, I set out on my pursuit of pleasure.

I plan breakfast for the first morning: Belgian waffles,

delicately toasted, covered in Vermont maple syrup, topped with fresh-picked strawberries and hand-whipped cream. I'll have orange juice flown in that morning from Brazil — all served by white-gloved waiters.

As I prepare for my feast, my anticipation couldn't be higher. I mean, this is going to be great. Just wait till I taste those waffles... The fluffiness, the gentle flow of sweetness, the depth of flavor — Heaven! I can't wait for the first bite. My mouth is watering just thinking about it.

And now I am there, the first morning of my pleasure excursion. I approach the table. My personal waiter pulls out the chair, and I sit down. The plate of food is brought in — covered of course, so that it arrives at exactly the temperature it came off the griddle — Heaven forefend for it to cool off while it is being brought out to me. The waiter sets it down, removes the cover, and...the first bite — wow! It is everything that I thought it would be. (Well, almost... I mean, they do taste very good.)

The second bite not far behind, as I concentrate on the aromas that waft through my palette, I focus on the balance of flavors and textures. Then the third bite, then the fourth... Then something happens... I find my mind wandering. I just start thinking about my day and everything else I have planned, and before I know it, I am almost finished the plate. Hey, what happened?... My waffles... the maple syrup... my personal chef... And I discover the first rule of pleasure: **The sizzle is better than the steak.**

▼

The First Rule of Pleasure

Did you ever notice that the restaurant ads show

a thick slice of meat about to be put on the grill, then SZZZZZZZZZZZZZZZZ! The smoke goes up, and you can almost taste the meat. Why don't they just show the cooked meat on the plate?

The answer is that one of the rules of marketing is: *sell the sizzle, not the steak.* Madison Avenue understands well that the *anticipated* pleasure is much greater than the actual pleasure.

Imagine how good it is going to be. Better than anything you have ever experienced. More delicious than anything you've ever tasted.

A funny thing happens when you actually bite into the dish. It isn't that the steak isn't good, and it isn't that the sizzle isn't real; it's just that the anticipation was far greater than the pleasure. *The sizzle is always better than the steak.*

The buildup is great, the anticipation is powerful — but the pleasure never lives up to the promise. Every pleasure is *over*-promised and *under*-delivered. The pleasure is built up to be the biggest and best thing that man has ever seen. And while the first bite *is* pleasurable, that pleasure quickly fades. Because the hype is always greater than what is delivered.

I Will Not Be Deterred

But I am a diehard pleasure-seeker, and a little touch of reality isn't going to put me off, so I continue on my journey. I finish my first helping, ask for a second and a third, and continue to enjoy a gala breakfast celebration.

Of course, no breakfast would be complete without dessert. Ah! A bit of Rocky Road, my private blend of ice cream, topped with hot Swiss chocolate and fresh whipped cream — only from

Hereford cows, please; their cream is just so much thicker.

And I lash into this with the same gusto. (Well, almost the same, because I am pretty full by now.) But this stuff is great; I mean, really great. The first spoon, the second, the third... And then I start slowing down as I simply run out of room. Hmmmmmm? And I suddenly discover the second rule of pleasure: **Every pleasure has a limit.**

The Second Rule of Pleasure

No matter what the pleasure is, it lasts for a finite amount of time, and then you are forced to stop. You can eat for thirty minutes, an hour, maybe even two hours, but then you are stuffed — there is just no more room.

Forget the hype, forget the buildup, and forget the sizzle being better than the steak. Let's take the pleasure itself. Assuming that it really is a deep, rich, memorable experience, how long does it last? No matter how great the pleasure is, if you count the actual time that you had "pleasure," you will find it to be very short, and then it is done.

Breakfast might last for an hour, but the actual time of intense and profound pleasure, when you were concentrating and taking in all the flavors and aromas, was probably only ten minutes if that long. Lunch might stretch out over an hour and a half, but the actual time of unique, dramatic eating enjoyment won't be much more than twenty minutes. If we throw in a candle-lit dinner set against the ocean backdrop, assuming that you aren't distracted by the company, the conversation, your own inner chatter, or whatever else pulls at you at that moment, you might add another twenty minutes. So we have racked up less than an hour of intense powerful pleasure.

And that is the second rule of pleasure: *Every pleasure has its limit.* Ten minutes, twenty minutes, maybe an hour — then it is done.

I Am Not Giving Up

But I am not giving up that quickly, I waited all these years to have some real pleasure, and I am determined to get it! But it's time now to settle in for the evening. After all, this pursuit of pleasure thing is not to be taken lightly: I need my rest. If I miss even an hour or two from my normal night's sleep, I might wake up cranky and tired and not able to enjoy much of anything. So, early to bed for me.

I wake up the next morning fresh and invigorated, ready to take on every pleasure imaginable. I stretch my arms as this deep sense of satisfaction and fulfillment fills me as I contemplate a meaningful and productive day of pleasure-seeking ahead of me. (Well, not quite. I do feel a bit empty and shallow… but nothing will stop me in the relentless pursuit of pleasure, so I set about my day.)

I sit down to breakfast on day two, ready to soak it all in. My white-gloved maître d' asks, "What will be your pleasure, sir?"

"Those waffles yesterday were truly amazing," I tell him. "Let's try them again, together with some nice white wine."

He brings them out, and they look as glorious as they did yesterday. The aroma, the crispiness, the tender inside — glorious. But when I bite into them something is… something is… how do I say this… I mean… they're different… They just don't taste the same as they did yesterday. I mean, they still taste good and all... but there is something missing...

And I have discovered the third rule of pleasure: *The first time is the best time, but there is only one first time.*

The Third Rule of Pleasure

Have you ever gone to a new restaurant and had an amazing meal? The food was fantastic, the ambiance was perfect, the presentation glorious — the balance of foods, flavor and aroma, an experience to remember. What happens when you go back the next time? Likely it's still good, maybe even very good, but never quite like the first time.

Whether it is the first time that you drove a car or the first time that you owned a home, the first time you make a big sale or the first time your child looked up and smiled at you — there is nothing like the first time. After that, it just sort of loses its kick. When a teenager first gets his driver's license, he will do anything to get behind the wheel of a car. The feeling of independence and power is exhilarating. Ask a person who has been driving for twenty years to describe his drive to work that morning. I doubt he will describe his fight through rush hour traffic as an experience worthy of poetry.

And that is the third rule of pleasure: *The first time is the best time, but there is only one first time.*

I Am Not Giving Up Yet!

To be honest, by this point, this pursuit of pleasures thing is starting to wear a bit thin, but my entire life, all that I have asked for is some good powerful pleasure — I'm not giving up now that I am finally here! If eating can't do it for me, then I will find other ways.

So, off I go to a carefree life of pleasures and enjoyment. First to the Mercedes dealership to buy a string of cars in every color of the rainbow. Next off to Africa for a hot air balloon ride over the Serengeti. Then to Paris to go bungee cord jumping off the Eiffel Tower. No expense is too great, no distance too far — the absolute pursuit of pleasure is my goal.

And I must admit, it is great! Wow! The rush of adrenaline as I looked down and watched a rhinoceros charging out of the undergrowth! (Well, it didn't really charge, but it did sort of walk, and I did have to hover for two hours in 115 degree heat till it finally decided to move.) That sense of excitement and exhilaration as I stared down a thousand feet to the concrete of the French street below! (Terror might be a better word, but I said to myself, "Yes, now *this* is truly living.")

But when it is all over and I come back from my exotic and far-flung adventures, I discover the fourth rule of pleasure: *I had a good time.*

▼

The Fourth Rule of Pleasure

Ask someone to describe a pleasurable experience, maybe a week-long cruise to the Bahamas, a ski trip to the Swiss Alps, and carefully study their description:

"Wow, it was amazing."

"I had such a great time."

"I enjoyed it so much."

Please note that all of these are in the past tense, as in:

"Wow, it *was* amazing."

"I *had* such a great time."

"I *enjoyed* it so much."

And so we come to the fourth rule of pleasure: *Once the pleasure is had, it is gone.*

Used up. No more. Nothing left but memories. I am left as I was before the pleasure — unchanged.

Universal Laws of Pleasure

The interesting part is that these rules show themselves in every culture and every time period. They seem to be an iron law of man's stay on the planet. All pleasures are limited and passing. They look so alluring, so tempting. It really seems that my life will be different, but the physical pleasures pass and I am left… the same.

What Are We Up To?

Now, as they say, the plot thickens. It is clear that Hashem wants us to enjoy life, as He created many, many pleasures, and gave us the ability to benefit from them. He also gave us the drive to seek them. Yet, for some reason all pleasures seem to be so limited, so difficult to attain, and so passing. Does He want us to enjoy them or not? If He doesn't want us to benefit from all of these features, why put them there in the first place? If He does want us to enjoy them, why is it so difficult?

Still, as puzzling as these questions are, they pale in comparison to the bewilderment we face when we analyze one more aspect of the way that Hashem made man.

CHAPTER 7

Let Us Make Man

ספר מסילת ישרים - פרק א

וְתִרְאֶה בֶּאֱמֶת שֶׁכְּבָר לֹא יוּכַל שׁוּם בַּעַל שֵׂכֶל
לְהַאֲמִין שֶׁתַּכְלִית בְּרִיאַת הָאָדָם הוּא לְמַצָּבוֹ
בָּעוֹלָם הַזֶּה, כִּי מַה הֵם חַיֵּי הָאָדָם בָּעוֹלָם הַזֶּה?
אוֹ מִי הוּא שֶׁשָּׂמֵחַ וְשָׁלֵו מַמָּשׁ בָּעוֹלָם הַזֶּה? "יְמֵי
שְׁנוֹתֵינוּ בָהֶם שִׁבְעִים שָׁנָה, וְאִם בִּגְבוּרֹת שְׁמוֹנִים
שָׁנָה, וְרָהְבָּם עָמָל וָאָוֶן" (תהלים צ, י'). בְּכַמָּה מִינֵי
צַעַר וַחֲלָאִים וּמַכְאוֹבִים וּטְרָדוֹת, וְאַחַר כָּל זֹאת -
הַמָּוֶת. אֶחָד מִנֵּי אֶלֶף לֹא יִמָּצֵא שֶׁיַּרְבֶּה הָעוֹלָם לוֹ
הֲנָאוֹת וְשַׁלְוָה אֲמִתִּית, וְגַם הוּא - אִלּוּ יַגִּיעַ לִמְאָה
שָׁנָה כְּבָר עָבַר וּבָטֵל מִן הָעוֹלָם.

*No thinking person could possibly believe
that Hashem created us for our station in this
world.*

Mesillas Yesharim, Chapter 1

If you look at the wondrous world we live in, it sure does seem that Hashem could have done a much better job at creating man. In fact, it seems that there is much good in this world that Hashem *intentionally* held back from man.

Let's start with the animal kingdom. There are many gifts that animals enjoy that man doesn't. If man is the highest order of Creation, wouldn't it make sense to take all of the strengths of the animal kingdom and invest them in him? Yet that isn't what we see. Let me give you an example.

You Can't Fight a Bear

George Dillman was a karate master. He was also a bit of

a showman. He decided he was going to put on the ultimate karate demonstration. He had already gone through the whole gamut of breaking things: first boards, then bricks, and then large blocks of ice. Now he was looking to do something really spectacular. He decided that he was going to fight a bear.

Of course, it was only going to be a show, so he hired a circus bear for the performance. The bear had been trained to wrestle, and George got together with the bear's trainer to choreograph a fight scene between "man and beast." Here, however, was the problem. While George may have been a highly proficient martial artist, he had a flaw: he took himself seriously — maybe a tad too seriously. He decided that he was going to make headlines. Instead of just going through the fight scene as planned, he was going to actually knock the bear out.

On the day of the demonstration, the crowd gathers and George takes the stage. The trainer brings out the bear. The two square off, and the "battle" begins. The bear moves forward, and George steps back. The bear lunges toward him, and George sidesteps. Then the bear swings wide, George ducks, and then he hauls off and smashes the bear full force in the chest. You could hear the thud three rows back.

Needless to say, George didn't knock the bear out. But he did manage to get the bear angry. Real angry. So angry that if it weren't for the bear's trainer somehow stepping in and calming the animal down, George would have been killed.

George learned an important lesson that day: you can be a high ranking karate master with twenty years of combat experience, but you can't fight a bear. A bear is six hundred pounds of solid muscle! A bear is just so much stronger than a man.

As Strong as a Bear

Here is a question to ponder: why didn't Hashem create us like bears? Why didn't Hashem make man big and strong and made out of six hundred pounds of solid muscle? Wouldn't it have prevented an awful lot of suffering over the years? Wouldn't man's stay on this planet have been more pleasant?

Have you ever waited for a bus on a freezing February morning and no matter how many layers of clothing you had on, you were still shivering to the bone? You won't find that happening to a polar bear. Polar bears have a layer of fat under their skin that keeps them warm. In the middle of winter, they break open the arctic ice and go in for a nice dip. Then they come out and sun themselves in the minus twenty degree air. Why didn't Hashem make us that way? Why not create us just like a polar bear, big and strong with a thick fur coat so that we shouldn't suffer from the cold?

Why not take the same essence of man — the same intelligence, the same personality — and put him into a stronger, more powerful body? Wouldn't man have been better off that way?

A Shark's Tooth

Let me give you another example. Have you ever found yourself in the dentist's chair in excruciating pain? The next time you do, I want you to think of the *shark*. Why the shark? Because that mighty hunter of the sea has up to twenty-five rows of teeth, one set behind the next. If one tooth gets damaged, another one falls into place. A shark is born with a lifetime's supply of teeth. Now, wouldn't it have been more convenient to create man that way, with many rows of teeth? If one goes bad, just pop it out, and in comes the next one.

Why didn't Hashem create man that way?

It seems that there are many advantages that creatures of the wild have that man was not given. He was created as is: weak, susceptible to attack, and subject to the elements. It almost appears as if man was purposely created in this *independent yet dependent* mode, as if he was to be the master of his fate, yet still fragile and vulnerable. And the question that begs being asked is: why? Why not make him big and strong and indestructible?

An even clearer example of this is disease and illness. Hashem created a stupefying immune system in man — ready to pounce on every imaginable germ — yet He left huge, gaping holes in that defense system. Take man, the powerful controller of his own destiny. Along comes one lone cancer cell, and our man is no more.

▼

The African Clawed Frog

Michael Zasloff, a biochemist with the National Institute of Health, recently made a fantastic discovery. While working with the African clawed frog, he noticed that it never suffered infections. Even when researchers performed surgery on these frogs and returned them to murky, bacteria-filled waters, they remained free from disease. Two months after making his observation, Zasloff discovered *why*. It seems that the frog's skin secretes a family of antibodies that protect it from infection. When the frog feels threatened, it emits a white fluid that kills all known forms of bacteria.

Isn't that amazing: a frog that can't get an infection? A small, insignificant creature that is impervious to disease. How many people have died of infection over the millennia? Before penicillin, it was probably the greatest killer on the face of this planet. And even now, don't we suffer from all types of infections and illnesses?

Why not put these same antibodies in man? We see that Hashem is capable of creating an organism that is completely protected from disease; He did it for the little frog. Wouldn't it have been kind to give this to man as well? Wouldn't man's stay on this planet be improved? Wouldn't he live longer and enjoy life more without the constant threat of sickness looming over his head?

If you were to tell me that Hashem wasn't wise enough to figure out all of the answers to man's problems, it would be one thing. But we see a world replete with His wisdom. We see these very wonders in abundance in the natural world. Yet man was given some advantages and not others. Doesn't it make you wonder?

What about Pain?

But there are other features that are even more problematic. It seems that there are some things Hashem put into man that do him no good at all. In fact, quite the opposite, they seem to make his existence miserable. Let's take pain for example. Have you ever had a headache that wouldn't go away? Or a toothache that didn't allow you to function? Who needs it? What benefit does it provide?

How about someone in chronic pain, the type of pain that doesn't allow him to do anything other than focus on alleviating the debilitating anguish consuming him? What good does that do?

Granted, some pain is beneficial; avoidance pain teaches you to pull your hand away from a hot pot so that you don't burn yourself. But what about arthritic pain that won't allow a man to leave his bed? What possible benefit is there in that? And so, why create it? And if it need be created, why not provide some kind of shut-off mechanism? In such a complex and sophisticated system as the one hundred billion cells that make up the central nervous system, I am sure that Hashem could have put in a timer that would stop the transmission of pain after, say, five minutes.

This question becomes far more troubling when you look at all of the varied sorts of pains that plague man. When you stub your toe, it hurts, and when you smash your shin, it hurts — but the *hurt* isn't the same. A toothache is very different than a burn on your finger. A migraine isn't the same as a pulled hamstring. Kidney stones don't feel anything like an upset stomach. Each segment of the body has its own sensitivities, and each sensation is unique: burns, scrapes, bruises, fractures, and cuts. And pain varies in intensity. Have you seen those pain charts they show the patients after an operation? On a scale of one to ten, how *much* does it hurt? From severe to mild, from chronic to acute. You could write poetry about the different shades, flavors and gradations of pain.

Who needs it? Who benefits from it? And here is the key question: why create it? If it just sort of happened, it would be one thing, but it was carefully planned. An astounding amount of detail went into making it work. Site receptors were placed in the fingertip. Neural pathways were arranged to move the electrical impulses up the body. The thalamus, that part of the brain that directs traffic, was designed to properly move the data. The interpretive part of the brain was fashioned to read the information and send back its determination, the electrical signal regulated and directed back down to the site of the injury. All for me to say, "OUCH!"

Who needs it? For goodness sake, why create it?

I'm in a Great Mood

While we are asking questions, here is something even more curious. Scientists are now able to measure the effects of certain chemicals on our moods. When I am happy, there is a chemical change in my brain and an increase in neurotransmitters that affect how I feel.

There are different ways to cause the release of these chemicals. One is via medication, and another is through exercise. After a sustained period of physical activity, a gland releases these chemicals, causing a sensation of mild euphoria. Athletes are well aware of this; they call it *runner's high.*

Here is a simple question: we know that Hashem is more merciful than anyone we could ever imagine. Hashem loves His creations far more than a father loves his child. So couldn't Hashem, in His infinite kindness, have given us a bigger gland that would constantly release this joy activator and we would be happy forever?!

Why not? It makes no difference to Hashem. He is creating the gland anyway; why not just make it a little bigger? That would put an end to so much misery in the world.

Imagine this: you wake up in the morning, stretch out your arms, and that gland secretes a nice big dose.

"Wow! How great to be alive!"

You sit down to a glass of orange juice, and another wave of euphoria comes over you.

"Wowwwwwww!!!!"

Why not create man that way? It is clear that Hashem has the capacity to do it. With this increased level of chemicals in his brain, man would truly be able to live a life of pleasure and comfort. Why not give it to him?

Let Us Make Man

To show you how penetrating this line of questioning is, let's say that I was given the opportunity to design man. At the risk of sounding irreverent, I think I would do a much better job than Hashem did. If I was given the chance to take all of the wonders that we see in this world and put them together to make a human being, I could put together man in a way that he would be much better suited for life in the real world.

Let's imagine early one morning, a booming voice from Heaven calls out: "RABBI!"

"Yes?"

"I HEAR THAT YOU HAVE MANY COMPLAINTS ABOUT THE WAY THAT HASHEM DID THINGS."

"Uhhh... No, Sir, not complaints. I just was wondering out loud..."

"IF YOU THINK THAT YOU CAN DO BETTER, THEN GO AHEAD. YOU MAKE MAN!"

And so, given a mandate, I set out to create man. Using

only features that I find already in this world, I get to pick and choose, putting together a brand new man.

------▼------

Superman

What a man I would make! I wouldn't create a puny, weak, little man. My man would be as strong and indestructible as a bear. He would be as fast as a cheetah and as brave as a lion. I would give him teeth like a shark and an immune system like the African clawed frog. He would have super-sensitive hearing like a bat, and he would be able to go for weeks without water like a camel. He wouldn't have a problem with pain. Not my man! I would give him an automatic shut-off switch.

But more than that, he would have a joy gland as large as a coconut. With a constant supply of joy, he would be as happy as a lark all day long. Oh, another thing. Laziness? Not in my man. I would give him the energy level of an ant. Why, he would work all day without tiring; only at night would he stop to rest. Anger? Nope. I don't think that would do him any good. I would get rid of that part altogether. What about competition and jealousy? Not a chance. Too many people have been killed over the millennia because of that. Arrogance? No way. He would be humble as pie. What a man he would be!

Here is the perplexing part: it is clear that Hashem is capable of creating just such a man, as He designed all of these features and placed them in other species. So why didn't He mix and match them, taking the best of each and blending them together to form the pinnacle of Creation — man?

The Way It Is

It seems that so much wisdom went into making man exactly as he is. It's as if Hashem purposefully created man in the state that he is in: strong, yet fragile; master of the earth, yet dependent upon it for his very survival. Man, who has the capacity to find joy, and also to suffer. Man, who lives with the full gamut of human weakness that entraps generation after generation, so often ending in war and destruction. Man, who is this unique conglomeration of strength and weakness, created in such fine balance. Why create him this way?

Summing It All Up

It seems that the more we study man, the less we understand.

It is clear that Hashem wants man to enjoy life, as He created many features solely for that purpose. Yet man doesn't seem to benefit from them. It appears that Hashem wants man to have pleasures, as He gave man an inborn drive to seek them. Yet when man does pursue them, not only does he find their enjoyment fleeting, he is left empty, yearning for more. It seems that Hashem wants man to be happy. Yet man has a host of conflicting needs and drives that leave him in an inner conflict.

However, by far the most bewildering point is that every improvement that man has over the animal kingdom seems to cause him only more unhappiness and more pain. Elsie the cow, grazing away in the field, doesn't suffer from depression. You don't read about mass suicide pacts amongst the lemurs.

If you search through the annals of time, what has man's wisdom brought him? Granted it has brought him love, altruism, a sense of caring and commitment to others. But it has also brought him jealousy, deceit, hate, war and destruction. Animals kill to eat. Man kills for a host of other reasons — with cause and without. If, on balance, most of humanity were happy most of the time, we might argue that man's lot was improved by adding these features, but that doesn't seem to be the case. In fact, quite the opposite — it seems that every feature given to man only causes him additional misery.

Why would a kind, giving Creator make man this way? Why would a loving God make life so difficult?

The answer to these questions isn't a one-line, pat response. Rather, it requires a dramatic perspective change. It calls for a different view of man and of what Hashem wants from him. It necessitates stepping out of our current existence, climbing up to 35,000 feet, and looking at life from a much broader vantage point. We are ready to start that journey.

CHAPTER 8

Understanding Life Settings

ספר מסילת ישרים - פרק א

וְנִמְצָא שֶׁהוּא מוּשָׁם בְּאֱמֶת בְּתוֹךְ הַמִּלְחָמָה הַחֲזָקָה. כִּי כָל עִנְיְנֵי הָעוֹלָם, בֵּין לְטוֹב בֵּין לְרַע, הִנֵּה הֵם נִסְיוֹנוֹת לָאָדָם, הָעֹנִי מִצַּד אֶחָד וְהָעֹשֶׁר מִצַּד אֶחָד, כְּעִנְיָן שֶׁאָמַר שְׁלֹמֹה (משלי ל' ט'), "פֶּן אֶשְׂבַּע וְכִחַשְׁתִּי וְאָמַרְתִּי מִי ה', וּפֶן אִוָּרֵשׁ וְגָנַבְתִּי" וגו', הַשַּׁלְוָה מִצַּד אֶחָד וְהַיִּסוּרִין מִצַּד אֶחָד. עַד שֶׁנִּמְצֵאת הַמִּלְחָמָה אֵלָיו פָּנִים וְאָחוֹר.

All of the situations of life, whether for the good or bad, are trials for man. Poverty on the one hand, wealth on the other.

Mesillas Yesharim, Chapter 1

R' Elazar bar Padas was one of the greatest Torah sages of his time. He was known as the "teacher in Israel." To his home came all questions large and small, to his address came all issues communal and personal. Yet despite the fact that he was a great individual, he led a very difficult life — suffering poverty, illness, and pain.

He was so poor that he often went without food. The Gemara gives us an example of a day in his life. One time, after undergoing a medical procedure, he returned home to a bare cupboard. He literally had nothing to eat. The only thing he was able to find was a clove of garlic. He bit into it and then passed out from malnourishment.

The word quickly spread that the great R' Elazar bar Padas was unconscious. The rabbis gathered in his house and waited. While he was in that state, they watched as first he cried, then he laughed, and then a beam of light emanated from his forehead.

When he awoke, the Sages asked him, "What was the meaning of all this: the *crying*, the *laughing*, the *beam of light*?"

R' Elazar bar Padas answered, "While I was unconscious, Hashem came to visit me. I asked Him, 'How long will my suffering continue in this world?'

"Hashem said to me, 'Elazar, my son, do you wish for Me to turn back the world to the first moment of Creation and maybe you will be born into a time of sustenance?'

"I said to Hashem, 'All of that and *maybe* I will be born into a time of sustenance?' Then I asked, 'Did I, at least, live half of my life?'

"Hashem answered, 'Yes, you already lived more than half of your life.'

"'In that case,' I said, 'return me to my current life.'

"Hashem said, 'The reward that you will receive in the World to Come is an estate so wide and so vast that there will be thirteen rivers running through it.'" (*Ta'anis* 25a)

Putting This into Perspective

There is much for us to learn from this incident. Let's begin with a question.

R' Elazar bar Padas was a great man. He was an enormous Torah scholar, one of the leaders of his generation, a man righteously following the ways of Hashem. By all accounts he was a *tzaddik*. Yet he was suffering, and not lightly — he was racked by poverty, pain, and illness. His plight was so difficult that when Hashem Himself came to visit him, the very first thing he said to Hashem was, *"How long will my suffering continue in this world?"* Wouldn't you imagine that Hashem's response would be, "Okay, you're a good man. You have done well. I will take care of you."

Not only wasn't that the response, Hashem said something rather puzzling, *"Do you want Me to turn the world back to the moment of Creation and maybe you will be born into a time of sustenance?"*

R' Elazar bar Padas wasn't asking for luxuries. He wasn't asking for riches and honor. He was asking for his basic needs, nothing more. Why didn't Hashem just say, "You have suffered enough. I will ease your plight."

To better understand this event, let's use a parable.

Actors on the Stage

Imagine that a famous actor gets a call from his agent.

"Listen, Jack, we just got a great offer. Tons of money, an all cash deal. You get the starring role, playing next to the greatest co-stars in the industry. But the best part of it is the plot; it's great. The story line really clicks. It's a guaranteed Tony. I'm sending the script over this morning. I want you to just sign off on the deal."

After reading the script, the actor calls back his agent.

"Bob, forget it. No deal."

"What do mean?"

"I mean it's no way. I won't do it."

"Jack, what is it? Is it the story line?"

"No, the story is fine."

"Is it the other actors?"

"No, they're fine too."

"So, Jack, what is it?"

"What is it? Don't you get it? The guy you want me to play is penniless and not too bright either. More than that, he's a jerk! I can't stand anyone seeing me that way."

"But, Jack, that's only the part you'd be playing. It's not *you*."

"Bob, forget it. Playing this part means everyone — the whole world — is going to see me as a down and out loser. I can't stand the embarrassment. Don't even ask me again, I'm not doing it."

And the actor hangs up the phone.

Judging an Actor

Obviously, this conversation never took place. Because any actor, as well as any person going to the theater, understands that those people up there on the stage are playing their parts. They aren't judged by how wealthy or poor they are in the production. They aren't rated by whether their role portrays a life of success or failure.

There is one criterion for judging an actor: how well he played his part. If his role is to play the part of an idiot savant and he does it convincingly, he will win accolades and praise. If his role is to be the most successful man in the world and he isn't real, the critics will rip him to shreds. He is there for one purpose — to play his role. He is given a certain backdrop and a certain set of circumstances. The character was born in this time period, has this type of personality, and has this amount of intelligence and charisma. Now go out there and play the part!

We, Too, Will Be Judged

This is an apt parable to life. Each person was given a specific set of circumstances and a particular set of abilities. The backdrop is set and we are given a role to play. Born into a particular time period, to a particular family, given a very exact set of parameters. You will be so tall, so intelligent, have so much of this talent and so much of that one. Now, go out there and do it! Live your life, ford those streams, cross those rivers, and sail those seas!

At the end of your days, you will be judged. But you won't be compared to me or to anyone else. You will be measured against the most demanding yardstick imaginable — you. Based on your potential, based on your God given abilities, how much did you achieve?

Whether you are smarter or richer or more talented than the next person is irrelevant. The only issue is: how much did you accomplish compared to what you were capable of?

All of the things that we put such emphasis on — money, honor, and talent — are all stage settings. They are props to be used; they allow us to play our part. But in the end we aren't judged by the part we played. When we leave this earth, they don't ask us, "*How much money did Hashem give you? How smart did Hashem make you?*" The questions are far more penetrating and demanding. "How far did you go with what you were given?"

There is no objective standard or single yardstick that everyone is measured against, and the measure of man's success isn't in absolute terms. The system is far more exacting. It is based on your talents and strengths, your abilities and capacities. The only question they ask is how much of your potential did you reach? Eighty percent? Forty percent? Twenty percent? How much of *you* did you become?

"Hashem, Give Me a 180 IQ"

We tend to take far too much credit for that which was given to us, and too much blame for what wasn't. No one woke up one morning and said, "Hashem, I think you should create me with a 180 IQ... No, make that an 80 IQ." "Hashem, I think I should be 6′2″, strapping and strong. No, on second thought, I would rather be 5′4″, puny and weak."

Our life settings have been chosen for us, and we have no input in the process. Smart or dumb, attractive or ordinary, talented or not. These are the backdrops against which we live our lives, the scenery and landscape that surrounds us. But they don't define us.

Just as our external conditions are set, so, too, is much of our inner makeup. Our temperament has been hard-wired into us at birth. Studies show that whether a child is bold or timid, extroverted or shy, can be determined at twenty-two months of age. It is simply the nature the child is born with.

Granted, a person can work on himself. He can learn to overcome weaknesses and change the level of some of his personality traits. But each individual was given a certain predisposition and tendencies at birth. These are part of the stage settings of his life. He was born into a role, and this is the backdrop against which he plays.

This concept goes a step further:

A Very Small Sefer Torah

I had the opportunity to speak at my son's bar mitzvah, and I told the story of a small *sefer Torah* that had been in the news then. It went like this:

Joachim Joseph was a twelve-year-old boy when Rabbi Dasberg approached him and said, "It will soon be your bar mitzvah, and I want to teach you to read from the Torah."

Joachim refused. He just didn't want to *lain*. Rabbi Dasberg was persistent. Still Joachim refused. In the end, Rabbi Dasberg persevered, and Joachim Joseph *lained* from a very small *sefer Torah*... in Bergen-Belsen.

At the risk of his life, Rabbi Dasberg had smuggled a small Torah scroll into the concentration camp with him. When he saw twelve-year-old Joachim Joseph, so close to bar mitzvah age, he wanted him to *lain*. So early one morning, before dawn, under the very noses of the Nazi guards, they gathered together a *minyan*, and Joachim *lained* from that *sefer Torah*.

After the bar mitzvah "celebration," Rabbi Dasberg made another request. He asked Joachim to take possession of the *sefer Torah*. Again, Joachim refused. How could he, a young boy, take responsibility for such a precious article?

"I'm an old man," Rabbi Dasberg pleaded. "I probably won't make it out of here. You are young — you will survive. I want you to take this Torah, and promise me that the whole world will hear about it."

In the end, Joachim agreed. He took the *sefer Torah*, and he survived. After the war, he settled in Israel and placed that *sefer Torah* in a closet in his apartment, where it remained.

Years later, Ilan Ramon, the Israeli astronaut, in preparation for his upcoming mission aboard the space craft Columbia, consulted with Dr. Joachim Joseph about certain issues relating to his assignment. After their discussion, the conversation turned to the *sefer Torah* in Dr. Joseph's possession. Ilan asked to take it with him when he went up into space.

The story had a tragic ending, as the Columbia exploded into flames upon its reentry into the earth's atmosphere. But the promise made fifty-seven years earlier was fulfilled when the whole world learned about the *sefer Torah* that was on board.

The Punchline

The reason I told this story to my son at his bar mitzvah was to make a point. "Did you choose to be born in the USA in the 1990's?" I asked. "Did Joachim Joseph choose to be born in the 1920's in Poland? Neither of you chose your life. But you had better believe that his life was vastly different than yours."

And that is the point — no one gets to choose. Each individual is born into an exact generation, into a given family, in a specific birth order, with a precise family dynamic. That might include a domineering older brother or a whiny younger sister. It might mean being born with a silver spoon in your mouth or into the grip of poverty. Introverted or extroverted, bold or timid, robust or weak, tall or short, handsome or not. With specific talents and abilities, and an exact level of intelligence, each person is placed into the ideal setting for him. Our lives fit us like a hand in a glove, with each situation custom-designed by our Creator for that individual.

When a person understands this, life itself is fair. If not, then it makes no sense at all. How do you explain why some people have it so easy and yet others have it so hard? Why are some people born talented and others not? Why are some people born crippled? Or deaf or blind? Why is there autism in the world? What about polio?

How do you explain two brothers? One leads an idyllic life; everything he touches turns to gold — he is successful in business, has a great marriage, and his kids love him. But everything his brother touches turns to mud. He can't earn a living. His marriage is a wreck, and his kids are miseries. You can't argue that they had different upbringings. They were born to the same parents, raised in the same house, and went to the same yeshivahs. Yet one leads an enchanted existence, and the other is a shlemiel.

Roles We Play

If our condition in this world really mattered, there would be no answer to these questions. If this world were the reason for Creation, then none of these situations would be fair. But that is the point: none of them matter; they are simply different life settings. We are but actors on the stage. Our role is to play our part — rich or poor, handsome or ugly, successful or not. We aren't judged by the part we play, but how we play it. The role is irrelevant. The props don't define us. The only thing that matters is what we do with our time on this planet.

When we leave this temporary existence no one asks, "So, nu, tell me. How did you earn your living? Did you at least make a lot of money? Did the world shower you with honor?"

No one cares. It just doesn't matter. And while this is obvious, it seems to be one of the most elusive concepts. So much of what we don't understand about life is based on why one person has it so good, and why Hashem didn't give that situation to me. Why? Why? Why?

If we fully understood that it is all irrelevant, the question wouldn't occur to us. Why was she given that creep as a husband? Why was I born into a divorced home? Why is it so easy for him to learn and so hard for me? If, at the end of our days, we would be given the same written entrance exam into *Gan Eden* (paradise), then these would be valid questions. But we aren't. We are each given our own exam, and the questions were hand-written for us — before we were born. This will be your given talent pool. This will be the stage setting of your life. This is what you are capable of accomplishing. How far will you take it?

Football Player Put Back into Flabby Tycoon's Body

There was a novel written a number of years ago that illustrates this concept. It opens when a young, professional football player is preparing for the upcoming Super Bowl game. He is riding his bike on a country road to get into shape for the big game, and he enters a long curving tunnel. Unbeknownst to him, a car is speeding into the tunnel from the opposite direction, heading directly for him.

The angel of death on duty that day is new to the job. He sees the crash coming and decides, "Why wait? Why make him go through the gore and the mess?" So instead of actually waiting for the inevitable crash, he takes the football player out of his body at the very last moment before the accident, and brings him up to Heaven.

However, the angel of death made a mistake. Any normal person driving his bike through that tunnel would have crashed and been killed. But this man was an athlete with highly keen instincts; he would have veered off at the last minute and not been hit. He should be alive. But it's too late. His body is buried; he is up in Heaven. What do they do now?

The Heavenly court meets and decides they have no choice but to send him back. To do that, they have to find someone whose time is up and put the football player back into that body. The closest they can come up with is a rich tycoon living in an exclusive mansion. So this athlete finds himself in the flabby body of a wealthy snob with an entire staff of butlers and maids. The cute part of the story is how he plans to get his sagging, pampered, new body into shape for the Super Bowl only weeks away. He gets the prim and proper servants to run football drills with him on the front lawn of the stately mansion as he practices his passes.

While this is a charming story, it illustrates a significant concept: that football player found himself occupying a body. He opened his eyes and found himself in a life.

That exact experience happened to every one of us. Hashem took us and hand-selected a life to be the ideal setting for us to allow us to grow. We were put into this body and told, "Go live your life!"

The Answer to R' Elazar bar Padas

This seems to be the answer to R' Elazar bar Padas. That was the ideal life's setting for him. He was given a very exact backdrop, perfectly designed to challenge him. It would allow him to reach his potential. But that life included poverty. Not because Hashem didn't have enough money, and not because Hashem wasn't concerned for his good, but because that was the perfect laboratory for his growth. Based on his inner nature and abilities, that was the best opportunity to allow him to reach his potential.

Great wealth is a life test. When a person is so wealthy that he doesn't know where to begin spending his money — that is a very difficult test. In that state, the human feels strong and independent. "I don't need anyone. I can buy and sell the world. I don't need my children. I don't need my wife. I don't even need God." For some people, that is the perfect stage setting to challenge them to reach their potential.

Just as wealth is a test, so, too, is poverty. When you are so poor that you don't know where your next meal is coming from, and somehow you just scraped together the mortgage payment, and that night you hit a parked car, and no one saw it… do you leave a note or not? That is a very real test. These *situations* aren't accidents and they aren't happenstance. They are orchestrated life settings.

The Perfect Setting

This is what Hashem was saying to R' Elazar bar Padas. "This is the perfect life for you. This is the ideal setting to allow you to grow. Do you want Me to reshuffle the deck, search for a life that doesn't include poverty and will still allow you to reach your potential? Maybe I can, and maybe I can't. Because this life is perfectly designed for you."

This concept is fundamental to understanding life. Hashem put us here for a few short years. We were given almost unlimited potential to grow and become the great individuals that we were destined to be. We were put into the ideal stage setting and given all the right tools for that growth.

However, to fully make sense of life we need to deal with that one question that should be the center core of our existence — why did Hashem create me?

לזכר נשמת הרב שמעון בן צבי הירש ע"ה
מרים עלא בת ר' ישראל אלעזר הכהן ע"ה   פאלק בן הערצקא ע"ה
Dedicated by Deborah & Louis Greenspan

CHAPTER 9

The Gym And The Spa

ספר מסילת ישרים - פרק א

כְּלָלוֹ שֶׁל דָּבָר, הָאָדָם לֹא נִבְרָא בַּעֲבוּר מַצָּבוֹ בָּעוֹלָם הַזֶּה, אֶלָּא בַּעֲבוּר מַצָּבוֹ בָּעוֹלָם הַבָּא. אֶלָּא שֶׁמַּצָּבוֹ בָּעוֹלָם הַזֶּה הוּא אֶמְצָעִי לְמַצָּבוֹ בָּעוֹלָם הַבָּא, שֶׁהוּא תַּכְלִיתוֹ. עַל כֵּן תִּמְצָא מַאֲמְרֵי חֲכָמֵינוּ זִכְרוֹנָם לִבְרָכָה רַבִּים כֻּלָּם בְּסִגְנוֹן אֶחָד, מְדַמִּים הָעוֹלָם הַזֶּה לִמְקוֹם וּזְמַן הַהֲכָנָה, וְהָעוֹלָם הַבָּא לִמְקוֹם הַמְּנוּחָה וַאֲכִילַת הַמּוּכָן כְּבָר. וְהוּא מַה שֶׁאָמְרוּ (אבות ב, טז), "הָעוֹלָם הַזֶּה דוֹמֶה לִפְרוֹזְדוֹר."

This world is a corridor to the World to Come.

Mesillas Yesharim, Chapter 1

In his book *The Vanishing American Jew*, Alan Dershowitz writes that he taught a course in Harvard Law School entitled, *Thinking about Thinking*. It dealt with major life issues: Creation, God, religion…

During a classroom discussion, someone raised a point. "The purpose of religion is to study God or to serve God. If we are rating the various religions, doesn't it behoove us to rate God?" And so, they set out to rate God. How did God do at this thing called Creation?

Before I tell you how God did, I will share with you some of the background. If you look around at this world, you will see many wonderful things. There are sunrises and flowers, love and friendship, kindness and hope. There is a lot of good in the world. On the other hand, there is suffering and pain, divorce and broken hearts, widows and orphans. There is a lot of bad in the world.

Therefore, taking everything into consideration, they gave God a B-.

Not an F. Certainly not an A+. On balance, God rates a B-.

Rating the Rater

If I were given the opportunity to rate our learned professor, I would award him a D… for dumb. Not for his opinion — we live in a free country, and everyone is entitled to his view — but a D for sloppy thinking, for taking things at face value, and not asking the critical questions that a honest, inquisitive person must ask.

To explain what I mean, imagine that I was to pull a pen from my pocket, and say, "You see this? Whoever designed this *toothpick* did a lousy job. Look! Who needs this clip over here? And this whole barrel thing inside doesn't do any good… And every time I get it right back between my molars, I get this blue, inky stuff all over my mouth. Whoever designed this toothpick did a lousy job."

This would be an example of careless thinking. Before you rate the manufacturer, you have to know what the product was made for. As a toothpick, it might be lousy, but as a writing implement it might be well-constructed. Before you rate Bic, you have to know what function *they* intended the object to be used for.

In the same vein, before you "rate" the Creator of the heavens and the earth, you had better have a very good understanding of *why* He created this world. What was His purpose? What does He want from man? If you attempt to rate the Creator before you understand why He created the world, you are going to come up with some pretty foolish ideas.

The Answer —
Why Hashem Created the World

The *Mesillas Yesharim* in Chapter 1 tells us the answer.

Hashem is the Giver. Hashem wishes to share of His good with man. The greatest good and the greatest pleasure that man can enjoy is being close to his Creator. Hashem created man to allow him to enjoy that pleasure. However, for man to truly enjoy this, he must earn it. It must be something that he worked for — not something that was given to him. The way that he earns this is by making himself as much like Hashem as a mortal can.

Hashem is perfect. By perfecting himself, man becomes more like Hashem and becomes worthy of being close to Hashem. Therefore, Hashem created two worlds: this world and the World to Come. This world was designed with the challenges, trials and situations that allow man to perfect himself. The World to Come was designed to allow man to enjoy the reward of his labors. In accordance to the level of perfection that man reaches here in this world, he is able to enjoy the presence of Hashem in the World to Come. This world is the corridor to the World to Come — which is the purpose of Creation.

Not an Addendum

With this short burst of clarity, the *Mesillas Yesharim* defines our existence and changes our perspective on everything. Two worlds — each with its role, each with its purpose.

The key point is that the World to Come isn't an addendum to life. It isn't an afterthought. It's *the* reason that Hashem created the moon, the sun, the heavens and all that it contains. It's the reason that He made man. It's the reason for life. If a person doesn't understand this he has little chance of understanding anything that goes on in this world. Because he hasn't stopped to ask that critical question: what did the Manufacturer intend it to be used for?

Is it any wonder that people have questions about life? They are looking at only half of the picture. The purpose of it all, the reason for it all, isn't in their vision. So, of course, the whole thing makes no sense. And they have many, many questions. Questions on God. Questions on the system. Questions on the justice of it all. Why is life so hard? Why is there so much suffering in the world? Why do bad things happen to good people? Many, many questions — and no answers.

All of these questions are built on one premise: life ends in the grave. When we die, it's game over. We're dead and no more. If that were correct, then their questions are valid. Life makes no sense. It truly isn't fair. However, once a person understands the reason for life, then all of these quandaries vanish like smoke.

The Gym and the Spa

To put this into an analogy, imagine that you are invited to an exclusive health club. You've never been there, but you know the layout. On the right side is the gym; on the left is the spa. The gym is the area where people work out. It has all of the exercise equipment: the elliptical machines, the weights, the treadmills. The spa is the place to relax. It has the sauna, the steam room, and the massage tables.

You decide it's been a stressful week, so you head straight for the spa. But by mistake, instead of turning left, you turn right and find yourself in the gym. You look around and see red-faced men everywhere, grunting and sweating. You let out a cry, "Who needs all this equipment? What's all this running, pumping and pushing about? Whoever designed this spa did a lousy job!"

This is an apt parable for Creation. Hashem made two worlds: This World and The World to Come. This World is the gym. This is where we work out, where we grow and become bigger and better people. The World to Come is the spa. That is where we enjoy the results of our work. Each world has its place, each world has its purpose. We were put in this world for a few short years to accomplish our mission. Then we leave it and enjoy our accomplishments in the World to Come.

This parable is so fundamental to understanding life that without it, nothing under the sun makes much sense. If a person attempts to make sense out of life without realizing that we were put on this earth to grow and then to enjoy our accomplishments in the World to Come, then he will find many, many questions that have no answers. Not questions that he doesn't know the answers to — questions that have *no* answers.

God Would Rate an F

In fact, if you assume, as it seems our learned professor

does, that life ends in the grave, then God wouldn't rate a B-. He would rate an F. An F for creating many things that didn't need to be there, and even worse, for designing many features that make man's stay on the planet more difficult.

Pain. Suffering. Hardship. Disease. Worries. Anxiety. Who needs them? Hashem created everything. There are no limits on Hashem, and no one telling Him how to do things. He is the one who created the pain delivery system, and He is the one who created the human personality. If Hashem so willed it, man wouldn't suffer. Not a little. Not a lot. Not at all. All pain would be wiped out.

Yet He purposefully created the means and manner to allow man to suffer. The question that begs being asked is — *why*?

The *Mesillas Yesharim* explains that the human condition *proves* the World to Come. If this world were the end all and be all of existence, then it would be true, Hashem did a terrible job. If it could be, Hashem blew it. But that is exactly the point: the reason for life is growth, and these features are all part of that odyssey. All of the tests, trials and tribulations of this world are the challenges that allow man to grow. All of the situations that we go through foster our development. Our position in this world — healthy or sick, rich or poor — isn't relevant. The only thing that matters is how we use this world — what we accomplish in the gym.

A Perfectly Imperfect World

Why it is that man suffers so? Why did Hashem design a custom-made world with such care and concern, yet purposely make it so hard for man to enjoy those features? Granted

Hashem made the orange, the pear, and the grape, but He also made man in a manner that it is very hard for him to enjoy these things. Why do it?

When we come to the core realization of *why* Hashem put us here, we view life very differently. Our station here isn't significant; it is a vehicle, and in that context it makes sense. We begin to see the form and the flow of this world. While we may not know the answer to every question posed by man, we have a framework to base our answers upon. The patterns of our experiences weave a tapestry of meaning and beauty. All of the questions melt away as reason and perception set in. The more time we spend on this journey of understanding, the more the pieces fit together. Once we get it, life itself makes sense.

However, to be successful at life we have to understand ourselves on a fundamental, core level. To know what is expected from us, what we are to change, and how the system functions, we need to examine the different parts of our personality, and the conflicting sides of our nature — we need to delve into the essence of man.

CHAPTER 10

The Animal Soul

ספר מסילת ישרים - פרק א

וְהִנֵּה שָׂמוֹ הַקָּדוֹשׁ בָּרוּךְ הוּא לָאָדָם בְּמָקוֹם שֶׁרַבִּים
בּוֹ הַמַּרְחִיקִים אוֹתוֹ מִמֶּנּוּ יִתְבָּרַךְ, וְהֵם הֵם הַתַּאֲווֹת
הַחָמְרִיּוֹת, אֲשֶׁר אִם יִמָּשֵׁךְ אַחֲרֵיהֶן הִנֵּה הוּא
מִתְרַחֵק וְהוֹלֵךְ מִן הַטּוֹב הָאֲמִתִּי.

Hashem has placed man in a situation where
there are many things that pull man away
from Hashem. These are the material desires.
If man is drawn after them, he is distanced
from the ultimate good.

Mesillas Yesharim, Chapter 1

When Moshe Rabbeinu went up to Heaven to receive the
Torah, the *malachei ha-shares* (ministering angels) tried to
stop him. Hashem told Moshe, "Explain to them why they
should allow man to have the Torah."

Moshe said, "When the three angels came to visit Avro-
hom, he served them meat and milk... and they ate it. Therefore, you must allow man to receive the Torah."

When the *malachim* heard this argument, they *immediately* agreed. (*Da'as Zekeinim, Bereishis*, 18:8)

Understanding this Midrash

Clearly, this Midrash presents a few problems. It seems

to imply that because three angels ate meat and milk, that proves that the Torah isn't for them, and should be given to man. How does that prove anything? First off, why is it a sin for a *malach* to eat meat and milk? Angels were never commanded to keep kosher.

Secondly, that event happened over four hundred years before Moshe went up to Heaven to receive the Torah. Why is it relevant that three lone angels ate non-kosher so many years earlier?

And, lastly, if an individual violating a Torah prohibition proves that the Torah isn't for that group, then surely the Torah should not be given to man. In the many generations since the Torah was given, we have to assume that a lot more than three men have eaten *treif*.

Why, then, is the fact that three angels ate meat and milk so potent an argument that "immediately they agreed?"

To answer these questions, we need to gain a better understanding of the very nature of man.

▼

The Nature of Man

The *Chovos HaLevovos* (*Shaar Avodas Elokim* 3:2) explains:

"Man was created from elements that are very different, whose essence are opposites, and whose very natures are in competition. They are his body and his soul. Within man, Hashem implanted drives and

ספר חובות הלבבות - השער השלישי - שער עבודת האלקים - פרק ב

מפני שנברא האדם מדברים שונים זה מזה, וטבעים מתגברים זה על זה, ומעצמים זה היפך זה, והם נפש וגופו, ונטע הבורא יתברך בנפשו מידות וכחות יכסף בהם לדברים, כאשר יתנהג בם האדם יגדל בהם גופו ויתחזק על יישוב העולם הזה, ויישאר המין האנושי על ענינו, ואם יפסדו אישיו, והמידה הזאת היא התאוה להנאות הגופיות, והיא כוללת כל מיני החי הגדל. והרכיב הבורא יתעלה בנפש האדם עוד מידות וכחות, יכסף בהם [אל דברים], כאשר ישתמש בהם, למאוס (ימאס) בעמידתו בעולם הזה ויחפוץ להיפרד ממנו, והיא החכמה (ההכרה) השלמה.

desires that are necessary for the continuation of the human species; these are all of the desires for physical pleasures. They are in man as in all animals. If man makes use of them, he will strengthen his physical standing, and the human race will flourish. In addition to these, Hashem implanted within the human soul strengths, which, if man uses, will cause him to look down on his position in this world and make him desire to separate from it. This is his spiritual part."

Within this short paragraph we have been given the formula for man's nature. When Hashem created man, He joined two diverse elements to form his living soul. These are his spiritual soul (what we call his *nishamah*) and his animal soul. The conscious "I" that thinks and feels is made up of both parts.

The *nishamah* comes from under the throne of Hashem's glory. It is pure and lofty, holy and sublime. All that it wishes for is that which is good, proper and noble. Because it comes from the upper worlds, it derives no benefit from this world and can't relate to any of its pleasures.

The other part of man's soul is very different. It is exactly like that of an animal, with all of the passions and desires necessary to keep him alive. It is his *animal soul*. If we wish to understand man, to make sense of what drives him and relate to what matters to him, then as much as we need to understand the *nishamah*, we need to understand this other part of man's soul.

Understanding the Animal Soul

An animal has a living essence. Just like man, it has a part that isn't physical. It is attracted toward certain types of objects and repelled by others. A dog will form attachments to its master and will even risk its own life to defend him.

As an example: When I was a *rebbe* in yeshivah, there was a fellow in the high school who had a difficult time going home for an out Shabbos. When he was a little boy, his father bought him a puppy. He and the dog grew up together, and it became attached to him. When he went away to yeshivah, the separation was very difficult on his dog.

When this young man would go back home every six weeks or so, his dog was very excited to see him, and would run out to greet him. The problem was that in its enthusiasm, it would go into frenzy, and relieve itself all over its master's pants leg! I don't think he was all that pleased with his pet's loyalty.

The point is that every animal has a part of it that is vibrant and living, and just like a human soul, this part isn't physical, but spiritual. When a dog sleeps, its body lies there flat and almost lifeless. When it wakes up, its essence comes back again. That part of the animal, its inner essence, is its *animal soul*.

Instincts Needed for Survival

Hashem implanted into the animal soul all of the drives the animal needs for its survival. A cat hunts mice by instinct. A bird eats worms because of an inner urge. It would be hard to imagine a robin thinking, "Based on my nutritional needs, as well as my capacity to hunt for, capture, and digest such foods, coupled with the general availability of such items, I have surmised that it would be best for me to utilize the worm as my food staple." The bird hungers for a worm. It has a natural pull, an inborn inclination toward its food.

Studies show that when animals raised in captivity are released into the wild, they instinctively hunt for the ideal food source for their species. When let loose, Siberian tigers that were orphaned at birth and brought up on bottle milk begin hunting deer, their natural food source, even though the tigers had never before seen a deer, let alone watched one being hunted down to be eaten. Inborn in them are the tools, the aptitude, and the inclination to capture and consume the types of food that best assures their survival.

So, too, with mating. Two bull frogs don't sit down to discuss their future, with one saying, "Kermit, I think it's time for us to settle down and raise a family." Hashem implanted into each animal all of the necessary drives for its survival as an individual, as well as the survival of the species as a whole. Those instincts and hungers are part of its animal soul.

Animal Soul in Man

Man, as well, has an animal soul. There is a part of him that yearns for physical things. He desires to eat, sleep, and procreate. Hashem put into man's animal soul all of the inclinations he needs to stay alive. If he follows these instincts, he will survive, and the species of mankind will continue.

The animal soul forms a part of me. The "I" that thinks and feels is comprised in part of these instincts and drives. Within me, there is a part that needs to eat. We wouldn't say my body hungers for food — I do. The essence of me desires food.

I am made up of both of these parts: pure spirituality and

animal instincts. I have a part of me that is more sublime than the angels, and a part that is as impulsive as any member of the animal kingdom. When a dog feels the need to procreate there is nothing that stops it: desire rules over the animal. I have that side to me as well. Within me is a set of instincts for physical activities and pursuits. The greatness of the human is that the other part of me, the part that is pure intelligence, can control the animal instincts. It can use those drives and passions properly, channeling them to productive and positive ends.

The Fight in Man

These two elements of man are opposites, and they fight for primacy and control over the person. As a result, man is in constant flux. The more he uses either side, the stronger and more influential it becomes. Much like a muscle that becomes stronger with use and atrophies with disuse, if a person uses his spiritual soul to control his animal soul, it becomes stronger, and he becomes elevated. If he gives in to his desires, then the animal soul gains command. His desires become more intense and frequent. They demand to be fulfilled more often and with more force — man becomes controlled by his drives.

In this regard, man's animal soul is different than what is found in the wild kingdom. An animal's desires are set to a certain intensity at birth. They will fluctuate based on seasons and circumstances, but all within a given range. Man, on the other hand, has less restriction on the intensity of his desires. If he controls his animal instincts, they lessen, so it becomes easier for him to dominate them. He becomes their master. If he allows them to rule, they become stronger and more extreme until they are in command. Then, man is but a puppet in the hands of his appetites.

Self Mastery

The process of living is a battle between these two forces. Ideally, if a person succeeds completely, his pure intellectual soul will harness his animal soul and use it for the purpose of keeping himself alive. Like a captain steering his ship by the wind, he uses the animal soul and its energy to accomplish his objectives and goals. When he eats, it is for the purpose of maintaining his health so that he can properly perform his mission on this planet. When he procreates, it is for the purpose of bringing children into the world and creating a harmonious, loving marriage. The pleasures that he takes from this world are also for a purpose: so that he should be composed and have peace of mind to be better suited to pursue his path.

By using the animal soul in this manner, not only does he increase the control that his *nishamah* has, he elevates everything that he does. Mundane, physical activities necessary for human survival are elevated into the highest forms of positive acts, and the human functions on the utmost level of spirituality — an angel in the form of a man.

However, if a person allows his animal desires to win and he follows their natural pull without controlling them, they become stronger and eventually rule over him. He is no longer able to make decisions based on wisdom. Rather, like an animal, he is dominated by whims and governed by passions until he loses control of himself and ultimately even the ability to choose. He becomes more animal-like and less God-like, eventually becoming nothing more than an animal in the shape of a man.

Dr. Jekyll and Mr. Hyde

This is the human: a walking, breathing, living contradiction, made up of two drastically different elements, completely opposite in nature. And so we find man acting in the most peculiar manner. Do you ever wonder how it is that we can find the same person acting in such contradictory ways? On one occasion, he is tolerant and understanding; the next he is inflexible and short-tempered. One moment he is benevolent and kind; the next he is as mean as vinegar. The strange part is that it's not some Dr. Jekyll and Mr. Hyde — it's me! Catch me in the right moment, and I am noble and distinguished. A minute later and I am a self-centered lout. What happened? How can I make sense of my own behavior?

We don't spend enough energy watching ourselves and seeing who we really are. We are so accustomed to explaining away our behavior in a favorable light that we lose the ability to see ourselves with an honest appraisal. The reality is that we have two sides to us, and depending on when you catch us and in what mood we are in, our reactions will vary in the extreme.

I could be sitting with someone in my study, having an inspiring discussion about the greatness of the human spirit, about elevating our lives, and the finest niceties in human behavior. We might go on for hours on end. Later on, I find out that this man went home, got into a fight with his wife, and began swearing, screaming and much worse. And I want to ask myself, "Is that the same person? Can the same human being who just an hour ago was involved in a discussion about the betterment of the human then go home and beat his wife?"

How do we explain it when driven people, powerful goal-setters who are extremely successful at what they do, throw away everything that they have — their career, their marriage, and their reputation — all for an affair with a secretary? If we claim to understand the very fabric of the human personality, how do we make sense of it?

Losing Control

The answer is that after giving in to his desires, man loses control. He becomes animal-like, ruled by desires and passions. Animals are governed by instincts. When the desire to mate hits it, no controlling agent holds it back. People who have owned a pet in heat will tell you stories of cats jumping through plate glass windows and dogs digging holes under garden fences. The animal is captivated by an uncontrollable urge.

Man, too, has urges and desires, but he has the capacity to control and harness them. If he does, then these drives, while still a part of him, become less powerful. They lessen in intensity and in the urgency with which they demand being fulfilled. When he gives into these passions without marshalling them, he effectively gives up control over himself. They grow and become more demanding, more incessant, and more potent. They begin affecting his judgment and decisions, exerting more and more influence and rule over him. Eventually, they become the master and he the slave, until he reaches a point where he will do things that are destructive to him and completely against his self-interest.

Throughout the process, he may think that he maintains control, but like a drug addict who needs a fix, the urge becomes so strong and demanding that it would take superhuman effort to resist it. The desires didn't start that way. At an earlier stage in his life, they didn't envelop him to the extent that they do now. It was a long process of "giving in" that allowed these desires to become stronger, causing him to slowly lose more and more control, until he found himself in a position in which he may almost not be able to stop them.

We humans are this contradictory combination. Within me is an animal soul made up of pure desires and appetites, and within me is a holy *nishamah* that only wishes to do that which is right and proper. The animal soul only knows its needs and exists to fulfill them. The *nishamah* is magnanimous and only wishes to give.

These two total opposites are forged together to create the whole we know as the human. Each part cries out for its fulfillment; each component vies for control. And so the human is in a state of constant change as one force or the other gains primacy. Is it any wonder that we find such varied and diverse behavior from a being whose very nature is at odds?

Why Create Man this Way?

Now we come to a critical question: why did Hashem create man out of such conflicting elements? Why form him in this state of constant inner battle?

The answer to this question is based on understanding the concept of free will. While free will sounds simple enough, it is actually one of the most brilliant features in all of Creation — and one of the most difficult to comprehend.

As an illustration: ask any young yeshivah student if an angel has free will. Can an angel choose to ignore Hashem's command? You will get an emphatic "No! Of course, a *malach* doesn't have free will. Everyone knows that."

Interestingly enough, angels do have free will. There are many places in Torah where we find that they are punished for not doing what they should have done. Angels, like us, have the ability to either listen to Hashem or ignore Him.

The distinction between a man and a *malach* is in their level of understanding. A *malach* fully comprehends the consequences of its actions. It sees that whatever Hashem commanded it to do is proper and right, and whatever Hashem warned it not to do is wrong. In theory, an angel can ignore that which it was commanded to do, but it won't because it sees this as damaging to itself and all of Creation. An angel disobeying Hashem is akin to you putting your hand into a fire.

▼

Putting Your Hand in a Fire

Imagine that I were to pull out a crisp one hundred dollar bill and offer it to you if you put your hand in a fire for a minute. Do you have free will to do this? In theory, you do. Nothing prevents you from doing it. You could do it, but you never would — because it would be foolish. You wouldn't do it for a thousand dollars or even for ten thousand dollars. It is self-inflicted damage, and that is something you just wouldn't do.

So do you have free will to put your hand into the fire? The answer is, in theory you do, but you never would. That isn't what the Torah means when it says that man was given free will. Free will doesn't refer to *theoretical* free will, the theoretical ability to do something that you never would do. It refers to *practical* free will, where both sides are tempting, legitimate possibilities, and you must choose between them. Then you can be credited with making the choice and shaping yourself. You have the option not in theory, but practically because either choice was a real possibility. You could have just as well gone left as right, but you chose and made yourself into what you are.

A *malach* has theoretical free will. It could violate the will of Hashem, but it never would because it sees that doing so is harmful to itself.

On the very rare occasion when a *malach* does disobey Hashem, it is because of an error in judgment. For instance, a *malach* may calculate that in a given situation, the slight to Hashem's honor is too great to bear, and taking action, it oversteps its bounds. The motive was selfless and pure — it acted out of respect for Hashem. But it miscalculated. A *malach* is punished, even for an intellectual mistake, if it acts improperly. However, these situations are highly unusual, and under normal circumstances a *malach* isn't even tempted to violate the will of Hashem because it sees the truth so clearly.

To Allow for Free Will

If man had been created with only a *nishamah*, he, too, would have had *theoretical* free will. It would have been possible for him to violate the will of Hashem, but he never would have. His *nishamah* is brilliant, insightful and wise. Intuitively, it understands that his Creator is good. Instinctively, it knows that every commandment that Hashem gave is for our good. So how did Hashem take man, whose wisdom is greater than the angels, and give him *practical* free will?

To do this, Hashem put this other dimension into man: the instinctual, drive-based part of him. Now part of man wants to do that which is good and proper, and part of him doesn't. Part of him wishes to live a life that is noble and lofty, and part of him couldn't care less. A full half of his essence is made up of appetites and hungers that can only care about the fulfillment of its needs.

Now man is pulled both ways: pulled toward a life of meaning and purpose and equally drawn toward the here and now. He is in utter, complete contradiction. His two sides are competing for control, each screaming out for its needs — each crying for its desires to be fulfilled. And now, he is in perfect balance, and has the *practical* ability to shape himself. It is his decision that determines which way he goes, and he can be credited for making himself into what he is.

The Torah — the System of Self-Perfection

The cost of this, though, is that it leaves man in a state of inner conflict. He finds himself locked in a constant struggle for control. He is in the battle called life. To allow man to win that battle, Hashem gave us a program for spiritual development, a means to strengthen the *nishamah* and bring it to the fore. That method is the Torah — the ultimate system of self-perfection. The Torah is the process and the guidebook that cultivates the spiritual side of man, allowing it to dominate the animal soul within him. It is replete with commandments and actions, many of whose meanings are readily understood, and others which take great depth to understand. But all of them with one goal: to empower man's spiritual dimension so that it becomes dominant. When man follows the Torah system, his *nishamah* is nurtured and energized, and he can tower over the angels, reaching the heights of greatness.

Forbidden Foods

This brings us to one of the most misunderstood elements of our religion: why the Torah forbids certain activities. The Torah commands us not to eat certain foods, not to wear certain garments, and not to engage in certain activities. Meat is fine. Milk is fine. But cook meat and milk together, and its forbidden. Linen is fine. Wool is fine. Mix wool and linen together and all of a sudden its *shatnez*, and you can't wear it. Why? What happened? What changed?

The *Chovos HaLevovos* (*Shaar Avodas Elokim* 3:2) explains that most of the mitzvos of the Torah are based on maintaining this fine balance in the human. Because these two parts of man, the *nishamah* and the animal soul, are at war, the Torah forbids certain activities because they give an unfair advantage to the animal soul. They strengthen it and give it extra force. Just as too much caffeine causes people to be jittery, anxious, and short-tempered, certain foods affect our spiritual balance.

Many commentaries explain that none of the kosher

animals are predators. We are forbidden to eat animals that kill their prey for food. Why? Because when a man ingests an animal, part of the *nefesh* (life source) of that animal is brought into him. We are commanded not to eat predators because doing so would bring those aggressive tendencies into us. Our animal soul would absorb these characteristics and it would affect the balances within us.

So, too, meat and milk cooked together strengthens the animal soul of man. To understand how it does that, you would need to be a scientist of the soul. That law is called a *chok* because the average person isn't schooled enough in spirituality to understand how it works. But the Torah warns us against it because it has the effect of making the animal soul more powerful and primary. The Gemara (*Yoma* 39) tells us that *treif* food deadens the heart of man. When a person eats forbidden foods, it becomes more difficult for him to feel the holiness of Shabbos, to learn Torah, and feel another person's pain. Why is this? Because in that fine balance of his personality, the animal soul has been strengthened, and by consequence his *nishamah* is weakened. The person becomes more animal-like and less God-like. And now, it is more difficult for him to relate to spiritual matters.

Fasting on Yom Kippur

Another example of this is the mitzvah to fast on Yom Kippur. Yom Kippur is arguably the holiest day in the Jewish calendar, and certainly a pivotal day in a person's life. Our entire future is decided on that day, and it is a time for repentance and change, growth and prayer. A person can reach dizzying heights on that day. Wouldn't you assume that we would be commanded to come to shul energized? Eat a good breakfast; it is a long day of davening and introspection, and you will need your strength. Yet that isn't what the Torah commands us to do. Quite the opposite, we are commanded to completely refrain from eating or drinking. Why?

Again, the *Chovos HaLevovos* explains that this is part of the system. When I fast, my body is weaker. The animal soul is dimmed, and it has less sway and control over me. I start thinking differently. Life takes on a different viewpoint, and my priorities start to shift. What used to be so important to me suddenly isn't. Those things that I pushed away now loom forward.

Around mid-afternoon, when the fast really starts to take effect, there is a noticeable effect — my body is now weakened. I feel differently than I normally do. The balance within me has changed, my perception has changed — *I* have changed. I now look at life from a different vantage point. I see things clearly. I can relate to my goals in life. I can focus on my purpose in life. I can ask myself that key question: am I accomplishing what I was put on the planet to do?

Answer for Malachim

This seems to be the answer for the *malachim*. The mitzvos of the Torah are designed as the system of perfection for man who has two parts to his soul. The mitzvos are focused on helping the *nishamah* win against its competing rival. Why did the three *malachim* eat *treif* food? An angel wouldn't sin. It sees things clearly. In theory it could sin, but it never would. The reason the three *malachim* ate non-kosher was because they were never commanded not to eat *treif* — non-kosher food doesn't damage them. They don't have an animal soul that gains primacy when they eat forbidden foods. Once Moshe Rabbeinu pointed this out, the *malachim* immediately admitted that the Torah was written for man. The mitzvos of the Torah were designed to allow man — this finely-tuned, highly balanced being — to perfect himself.

Understanding how the mitzvos function requires a deep knowledge of the two elements of man's personality and the interplay between them. Part of that process requires studying the animal soul in its natural element and then extrapolating to man. However, before we do that, we need to gain a better understanding of the holy part of man — that part that drives him to everything great and lofty — man's *nishamah*.

CHAPTER 11

The Princess
And The Peasant

ספר מסילת ישרים - פרק א

אִם תַּכְלִית בְּרִיאַת הָאָדָם הָיָה לְצֹרֶךְ הָעוֹלָם הַזֶּה,
לֹא הָיָה צָרִיךְ מִפְּנֵי זֶה שֶׁתִּנָּפַח בּוֹ נְשָׁמָה כָּל כָּךְ
חֲשׁוּבָה וְעֶלְיוֹנָה שֶׁתִּהְיֶה גְדוֹלָה יוֹתֵר מִן הַמַּלְאָכִים
עַצְמָם, כָּל שֶׁכֵּן שֶׁהִיא אֵינָה מוֹצְאָה שׁוּם נַחַת רוּחַ
בְּכָל עִנּוּגֵי זֶה הָעוֹלָם.

*If the purpose of man's existence were only
for his station in this world, it would not
have been necessary to place within him a
nishamah that is so lofty that she is greater
than the angels, especially as she derives no
benefit from all of the pleasures of this world.*

Mesillas Yesharim, Chapter 1

In the times of castles and moats, there lived a princess.
An only child, her life was to be one of comfort, lavishness
and splendor from the cradle to the grave. She wore only
satin and silk. She was served only the finest delicacies. She
lived an enchanted existence until her twentieth year.

One day, the princess went for a walk in the woods and
lost her way. Wandering for hours on end, she realized that
she couldn't find her way back to the castle. Exhausted, she
lay down on the bare ground and fell asleep. She dreamed
that she would never make it back home, that she was destined to spend the rest of her life in the woods.

She woke up with a start, looked around, and realized that
it wasn't just a dream; she was still in the forest. In a des-
perate panic, she ran — bumping, crashing, falling down and
getting back up again. Hour after hour, she ran deeper and
deeper into the forest... and further and further from the

castle. Exhausted, she collapsed and again fell into a deep slumber. When she awoke, she realized that if she didn't eat, she would die. She remembered that some of the berries and roots in the woods were edible, so she scrounged together some sort of nourishment and passed the time. Soon the days turned into weeks, and the weeks turned into months.

She Finds a Shack

After more than a year, her clothes tattered, her hair disheveled, she stumbled onto a clearing in the forest and saw what looked like a shack made of logs. She approached, slowly, cautiously... There were no sounds.

Silently, she circled the shack. It was empty. She opened the door, looked in, and saw a well-tended, primitive home with a table, chairs, and a fireplace. It looked like someone had recently been there. In the corner sat a wood-framed bed with straw for the mattress. Exhausted, and not having slept in a bed for over a year, she lay down and immediately fell into a deep slumber.

Many hours later, she awoke with a start, and saw a peasant standing over her. He was large, coarse, and darker than any man she had ever seen. But as shocked as she was to see him, he was equally taken aback by her presence.

A thousand thoughts raced through her mind. "Will he harm me? Who is he? Does he speak my language?" Before she had a chance to utter a word, he brought her a blanket and covered her with it. Out of absolute exhaustion, she fell back asleep.

When she woke up in the morning, she realized that she was alone again. The man was gone. She looked around the shack with its dirt floor, holes in the walls, and simple wood table and chairs. "It has almost a cozy look to it," she thought to herself. Slowly wiping the sleep from her eyes, she noticed a bowl of warm porridge on the table. Famished, she wolfed it down.

Her eyes filled with tears as she thought back to what were now distant times — to her home, the castle, bedecked with the finest ornaments; to her wardrobe, made of the most delicate fabrics; to her bedding, the smoothest satin and silk. She got up and wandered outside.

The smell of spring was in the air, and freshness seemed to hang in the clearing. She stretched her arms and took in the sweet smells. When she opened her eyes, she realized the peasant was there — standing at a distance, watching her.

He slowly approached.

He opened his mouth to speak. It was her language, but crude and broken. He was a simple man — uneducated and unrefined. He was, however, kind. Every day, she found her food prepared, and every day he returned from the forest bearing gifts — one day flowers, the next day a bowl carved from wood.

Time passed, and she began to feel almost at home in this hovel. She even felt herself somewhat attracted to this man. She remembered that first night in the woods when she dreamed that her destiny was to spend the rest of her days in the forest. Slowly she made peace with her fate. Within a short time, they married.

Her life in the forest is most difficult. She spends her days weaving, sewing, peeling and cooking — everything done by hand. And the winters are so harsh: bitter and unending, month after month of frigid cold, and she must wear the coarsest of garments that scratch her skin, yet barely keep out the cold. The only source of heat in the cottage is the fire that dies down after a few hours. Most nights, she wakes up shivering in the cold, and then her mind turns back to her youth, to the life of splendor and luxuries that she always thought would be her future.

What makes it even harder is that while her husband is good to her, none of the things that he brings her makes her happy — they just don't mean anything. He carves some beads, puts them on a string, and gives them to her, but her mind travels back to the pearls and diamonds that she wore long ago. He cooks some oats mixed with herbs for her, and she remembers the servants carrying in tray after tray of delicacies. Every gift fills her with melancholy as it pulls her back to an earlier life.

A Parable to Our Lives

The *Mesillas Yesharim* explains that this is a *mashal* (parable) to our lives. Part of me is the princess; part of me is the peasant. Each has its needs; each has its purpose. Part of me is a holy spirit that only seeks that which is noble, right and proper. It came from under Hashem's throne of glory, where it enjoyed the most sublime existence. Being of pure intelligence, it desires only to be generous and giving. It aspires to greatness. It was put into this world on a mission and it recognizes the importance and significance of life. Everything great in man comes from this part.

But there is the other part of me: the peasant. It too has desires; it too has needs. It is made up of all of the instincts and drives found in the animal kingdom. This part has no wisdom or self-control; it is comprised of hungers and appetites. It was programmed with all that man needs to keep alive and functioning in this world.

The conscious I, the part that thinks and remembers, is made up of both of these parts — the princess and the peasant. The reason that man has such difficulty achieving peace of mind is that both spirits move him in opposite directions — each pulls toward its own nature. The *peasant* part of man's soul desires everything that is here and now. It is simple. It can't see the future. It can only relate to that which is revealed and obvious. Based in the physical world, all that it knows are things of a material nature. Give it a place to sleep and something to eat, and it is happy.

Nothing Satisfies the Princess

The other part of me, the *princess*, desires so much more. She finds no satisfaction from anything in this world; she views all luxuries and material possessions as cheap tinsel. She finds every pleasure of this world coarse and unattractive. Bring her all the money that money can buy, and still she remains unmoved. It means nothing to her because she comes from a much higher place.

This part, the *nishamah*, also hungers — but not for food and drink; it hungers for meaning and purpose. It wants to grow, to accomplish, to change itself and the world it lives in. More than anything, it craves a relationship with its Creator.

Do you ever wonder why man just can't seem to find happiness? He runs after things, working so hard to acquire them, but when he finally gets them, they just don't mean anything to him. Why can't he just be satisfied with what he has? He sure pursued it hotly. He went after it like it was the answer to all of his problems. Now he has it, and he needs more. Why?

When people don't understand their basic makeup, they have little chance at achieving inner peace and harmony. They pursue many things thinking, "This is what I have been lacking. This is what I need. Once I get this last final thing, then I will be happy." But it doesn't work. It can't work because it only fills half of them. The other half is left hungrier than before. The peasant doesn't need much — a table and chairs, a simple shack and some bread, and it is good to go. It is the other part of man's soul that isn't satisfied — it can't be satisfied with anything physical.

I Am Both

One of the most elusive thoughts that seems ever to escape us is that *I* am a combination of these two elements. The conscious I, the part that thinks, feels, and remembers is comprised of both components. I am the princess, and I am the peasant. And because there are two sides to me, I desire very conflicting things. One moment I desire everything good and proper, and the very next moment, my entire focus is on things base and empty.

The strange part of it all is that I am normal. I don't have multiple personalities. I am a fully functional, sane human being. That, however, is the point. I am a human, and that is the way that Hashem made us humans.

Until a person comes to grips with these two parts of his personality, he won't understand what makes him tick, and his own motives and drives will remain a mystery — even to him. Once he focuses on these two parts of "I," then everything makes sense. The utter contradictions that make up our desires, the conflicting interests and needs that we experience, the competing sides to our nature, all come from this duality — the two parts of me.

Just as the peasant cries out for food and drink, the princess cries out for meaning and purpose, and for that reason we have such a difficult time enjoying this world. When a man lives his life in one dimension, filling his belly and then his pocketbook, the princess looks down her nose and says, "This is what I came to this world for? This is what life is all about?" And she lets him know her lack of satisfaction in very clear terms. She gives him no rest.

Drinking When You Are Thirsty

In a memoir written many years ago, a teenager describes what life was like for him growing up in the 1920's in the deep South. Hunger was a part of life; it was just a given. He got up in the morning hungry, and went to bed even hungrier. Often, he left home in the morning without eating breakfast, because there was no food in the house — literally nothing to eat.

One morning while walking to work, he passed a neighbor's house and noticed that the garden hose was left out. He turned on the spigot and began drinking and drinking until he filled his belly, hoping to stop the hunger pangs. It worked. His stomach no longer grumbled for food... till the water passed. Then he was left hungrier than before.

For many people, that is life. They feel emptiness inside, a longing for something. What it is they can't quite tell you, but it gives them no rest. They try to fill it with money and honor, possessions and luxuries, all the while hoping it will satisfy that void inside.

But it doesn't work. For a while they are distracted, for a moment their attention is diverted, but then the quiet time comes again, and they find themselves as empty as before. And the worst part is that for the life of them, they can't figure out why. "I have so much, yet I feel so poor! What's wrong with me? What's wrong with life?" The problem is that they are trying to fill their souls with things that sparkle and shine, but are as fleeting as fireworks on the fourth of July.

The princess within me isn't satisfied and can't be satisfied with anything so cheap, so she calls out for more. Instead of heeding her call, many people try to fill that vacuum with more glitter and gold. But the princess isn't impressed. So while they fill their bellies for a time and forget their pain, that gnawing hunger comes back to haunt them even more acutely than before.

I Need More

"But what's wrong? What am I missing? I thought I had it all. I guess I just need more." Then in a headlong rush to quell that vacant feeling inside, they pursue careers and promotions, honor and prestige, acquisitions and hobbies, distraction after distraction, running, running, running — anything, just to not think about the emptiness inside. From cars to homes, planes to cruises. Buy a boat, then a yacht. Next a Rolex, then a Rembrandt. Luxuries, parties, extravaganzas… anything, anything to fill that void inside. But it never works. They wake up in the middle of the night and mouth the words, "There has to be more to life than this."

There is. There is so much more. But if man doesn't

search for it, he won't find it. And if he doesn't find it, he is destined to be miserable. Living as poor as a blind mouse in a food silo, not knowing which door to open to find a treasure of provisions, right there for the taking — if only he would see it.

To achieve happiness and peace of mind, man has to know that he has a soul, and then he has to know what *it* needs to be satisfied. Ironically, this is something that even people from secular backgrounds have come to understand.

Victor Frankl — Man in Search of Meaning

Victor Frankl was one such person. A Viennese psychiatrist, he was a secular Jew who barely knew that he was Jewish. The Nazis made his identity clear to him when they deported him to a concentration camp.

After the war, he wrote a book entitled *Man's Search for Meaning*. The book has two parts. The first is about life in the concentration camps. He describes how he attempted to step out of the day-to-day existence and analyze life in the camps from a dispassionate standpoint. It is a harrowing read.

The second part of the book is equally telling. In it, Frankl describes what life was like for him after the war. After spending time in the displaced persons camp, he landed in the United States and opened a practice on the upper east side of Manhattan. As he had been a world-famous psychiatrist, he put out his shingle, and his practice was quickly filled. He explains, however, that the cases that he was now dealing with were unlike any that he had ever seen before. A woman would come into his office, and he would conduct the intake interview:

"Ma'am, how can I help you?"

"Well, Doc, I'm depressed."

"I see. Is it your marriage?"

"No. That's going well."

"Is it your kids?"

"No, they're fine."

"Is it work?"

"No, that's fine too."

"Well, what is it? Why are you depressed?"

"I don't know, Doc. That's why I'm here."

He describes that patient after patient would come in, depressed, but without any attributable cause. No trauma. No loss of a loved one. No loss of a job or income. His conclusion: these people were depressed because they lacked meaning in life; they lacked direction and purpose. A forty-five-year-old man would wake up and say to himself, "I am doing great. Making lots of money, my company is flourishing, but what is it all about? Why do it? What is the purpose of it all?"

Victor Frankl's conclusion, from a psychiatric vantage point, is that man without meaning will be depressed, and in fact, should be depressed because at the core of his essence he is empty. The only hope for him is to find meaning and purpose in his life. Only then will he achieve happiness.

Why Can't Man Be Satisfied?

He is correct. The reason is that Hashem made man for a higher purpose and gave him a *nishamah*, which won't let man settle. It won't allow him to be just mediocre. It makes demands of him. It demands living life with a purpose, it demands giving to others, it demands making significant contributions, and if its needs aren't met, it leaves him unhappy and haunted.

One of the paradoxes of life is that you can have everything and be poor, or have nothing and be rich. But it isn't only about attitude. It isn't simply an issue of appreciating what we have. It goes much deeper than that, cutting into the very fabric of the human personality.

Man has two sides to him. When he meets the needs of both, he achieves a state of balance and harmony. He is at peace with himself. When that comes about, everything is beautiful. The sun is shining, the birds are singing, and everything is wonderful. It may be raining outside, and you can't pay your mortgage, but it is okay, because things have meaning. You understand life. You understand what you are doing here. And you experience true joy and fulfillment. You are happy.

The purpose of life isn't happiness, and the Torah isn't merely a "self-help happiness guide." But a direct outcome of leading a Torah lifestyle is that you will be happy. The Torah is the guidebook to living a successful life. It was written by the only One who truly understands man — his Creator. When a person follows its ways, he is at peace with himself. Both the peasant and the princess have their needs met, and the person is in sync with himself.

Allowing the Peasant to Rule

However, when a person doesn't follow the Torah's guidelines for success, he invariably allows the peasant to rule. For a while it is okay; he is busy making his fortune and having fun. But part of him is unhappy and he just can't enjoy life —

no matter what he has, no matter how good his lot. All of the possessions in the world, all of the beauty in Creation, mean nothing to him because at the core of his essence, there is a voice inside screaming out its dissatisfaction.

"But, why aren't I happy? Why don't I feel fulfilled?" Just asking the question is as telling as the answer. Hashem created us for a destiny that is greater than simply getting on, making a living, going about this thing we call life. And because of this, I can't be satisfied with just passing time. I need more. Not more money or luxuries or cars. More meaning. More substance. More significance. Part of me is saying, "I can't believe that Hashem put me on this planet just to do the insignificant things that I do. There has to be a higher purpose. There has to be some meaning to it all."

If a person wants to live a meaningful, satisfying life, he needs to understand himself. He must relate to the needs of his soul. The only way that he can do this is by finding his mission in life, finding out why Hashem created him, and why Hashem put him into this thing we call life.

The Activity that Brings Man the Most Happiness

Once a person understands himself, he can engage in the experience that brings him the most happiness — growth. That is what Hashem put us in this world to do. That is the purpose of all of Creation. And Hashem implanted within us all of the drives and instincts that we need to grow.

The challenge of life is that there is the other part of me. There is the peasant who calls out with his needs, desires, and wishes. If a person follows that voice, for a while he is occupied, for a moment he'll find some satisfaction, but it quickly leaves him more empty than before.

Hashem Wants Us to Be Happy

Hashem wants us to be happy. Hashem created everything to give of His good to us. Even though the purpose of life is our station in the World to Come, Hashem wants us to be happy in this world as well. For that reason, He created so many amenities strictly for us to enjoy. But to enjoy them, a person must learn to use this world properly.

When man follows the Torah's path, he grows, he accomplishes, and he achieves his purpose in Creation — and he is happy. In that state, he can enjoy all of the beauty of this world. It doesn't distract him; it is a tool that he uses to further serve his Creator and enhance his growth. The challenge of life is not to get lost, not to get so caught up on the here and now that we forget that there is a tomorrow.

לעילוי נשמת
חיה דבורה בת אברהם ע״ה
Yaakov Katan

CHAPTER 12

Travel Brochures And The World To Come

ספר מסילת ישרים - פרק א

עַל כֵּן הוּשַׂם הָאָדָם בָּזֶה הָעוֹלָם בַּתְּחִלָּה, כְּדֵי שֶׁעַל יְדֵי הָאֶמְצָעִים הָאֵלֶּה הַמּזְדַּמְנִים לוֹ כָּאן יוּכַל לְהַגִּיעַ אֶל הַמָּקוֹם אֲשֶׁר הוּכַן לוֹ, שֶׁהוּא הָעוֹלָם הַבָּא, לִרְווֹת שָׁם בַּטוֹב אֲשֶׁר קָנָה לוֹ עַל יְדֵי הָאֶמְצָעִים הָאֵלֶּה. וְהוּא מַה שֶׁאָמְרוּ זִכְרוֹנָם לִבְרָכָה (עירובין כב, א), "הַיּוֹם לַעֲשׂוֹתָם וּמָחָר לְקַבֵּל שְׂכָרָם".

Therefore, man was placed in this world first, so that via the media he finds here he can acquire his place in the World to Come.

Mesillas Yesharim, Chapter 1

"Jamaica: White beaches, cloudless skies, endless oceans. Once you go, you know."

—*Travel ad*

There is an entire industry dedicated to writing travel brochures. Their advertisements offer to take you by rail, cruise, and camel back from the African rain forests to the snow-covered Alps. Then off to Jamaica, Aruba, and the Gulf of Mexico — from the quaint to the spectacular, the picturesque to the breathtaking. They beckon you to see the world.

If you watch people when they look at these pamphlets, they often get a far-off gaze in their eyes as they imagine themselves traveling to those exotic lands. This is interesting because most people who pick them up have no intention of ever going to those places. They're nice to look at, interesting to see, but it has nothing to do with me.

This seems to be the way we view the World to Come. Intriguing! Fascinating! I love the descriptions. But it has nothing to do with me. Don't get me wrong; being close to Hashem and enjoying eternal bliss sound wonderful. It's just that I have no intention of being there. You see, by the time it happens, I will be dead. My *nishamah* might be there. My soul could end up there. But me? I will be dead and gone. So this whole discussion is interesting, but irrelevant.

I Am a Physical Being

The reason we feel this way is that we view ourselves as *physical beings*. After all, isn't man just flesh and blood, a mere mortal? "With the sweat of his brow he earns his daily bread, and then passes from the earth never to be heard from again." We get so caught up in this limited definition of man that we start to believe it. And we start to confuse ourselves with our bodies. Oh, granted, I have a soul — whatever that is — but it has little to do with me. I am this body. Ever since I can remember, I've been inside this body. Everything that I have ever experienced is through it. I guess this is all there is. And life seems to confirm this. If you punch my arm, it hurts *me*. If I stub my toe, *I* feel pain. I and my body are one. So obviously, when this body is buried in the ground, I am dead. Gone. Extinct. And the World to Come is irrelevant.

Of course, we are *supposed* to believe otherwise. The problem is that in our heart of hearts, this is how we feel.

The question is: how do we get our feelings in line with our beliefs? Here is an illustration that may help.

———◆———

Near Death Experiences

In 1975, Raymond Moody caused a major stir in scientific circles when he published *Life After Life*, a book that chronicles hundreds of *near death experiences* — a term that he coined. In a near death experience, the patient is clinically dead, but is then revived and able to describe what "death" was like. Almost all of the cases share an eerie similarity. Typically, there was no heart rate, no respiration, and no brain wave activity, yet the person was conscious, aware and watching as attempts were made to resuscitate him. Often the patients described a sense of popping out of their bodies and hovering near the ceiling, looking down on the accident scene, while their bodies were pronounced dead. When revived, they were often able to relate detailed information about what transpired while they were "dead." Some repeated conversations verbatim. Others recounted in vivid detail the medical procedures attempted on their lifeless bodies — all done while they lay there unconscious, stone dead.

Since the publication of the book, thousands of near death experiences have been reported, and the subject has undergone much discussion and scientific study. The evidence seems irrefutable. Over and over, people come back and recount seeing things that they couldn't possibly have seen and knowing things that they couldn't possibly know because they were dead when they happened. To many, these findings challenge their understanding of life.

An Electric Toothbrush

The Lancet, a prestigious medical journal, reported on a recent landmark study that recorded a number of near death experiences that are highly illustrative. One involved a thirty-six-year-old woman who suffered an aneurysm and was bleeding inside her head. The normal procedure would call for the surgeon to open her skull and cauterize the area, burning together the ripped veins to stop the bleeding. The problem was that in her case, the injury was so deep in her brain that if they went in that far, the incision itself would cause so much residual bleeding that she would die from the blood loss. There was nothing they could do for her. They sent her home to die.

One surgeon offered hope. He had developed a technique to drain all of the blood from her head. By doing this, they could then go in and seal the damaged veins without causing bleeding. Once her skull was sewn back up, they would re-insert her blood. The procedure was experimental — there were no guarantees — but there were no other options, either. She consulted with other medical professionals. She met with her family and clergy. And she decided to go ahead with the operation.

On the day of the procedure, they put tape over her eyes and placed audio devices in her ears to ensure that her brain would not receive any stimuli that would cause it to draw blood. They placed her under anesthetic and submerged her body in a bath of ice to bring down her core temperature. When her body was cold, they drew out all of the blood from her head. The surgeon opened up her skull. He went in, found the damaged area, sealed it off, and closed her back up. They then re-inserted her blood, took her out of the bath of ice, and began the slow process of bringing her back.

She survived. While recuperating, her surgeon came to visit. She said to him, "Doctor, I must share this with you. While you were operating on me, I had this strange hallucination. I dreamed I had popped out of my body, and I was there in the room, up by the ceiling, hovering, watching. It was so strange. First I saw you take an electric toothbrush and try to put it into my thigh. I heard you say to the nurse, 'It's too small.' 'Try again,' she said. You tried. And again you said, 'It's too small.' The nurse said, 'Try again.' You tried again and you got the toothbrush into me. Isn't that strange?" the woman said, laughing.

The doctor didn't laugh. What she described had an uncanny resemblance to what happened in the operating room. Part of the procedure involved inserting into her thigh a medical instrument that from afar looked like an electric toothbrush. During the procedure, the doctor realized that her veins were too small, and he couldn't insert this instrument. He said to the nurse, 'It doesn't fit.' She said, 'Try again.' He tried again, but it still didn't fit. She said, 'Try again.' He tried again, and that time he was able to get it in.

The disquieting part was that all this happened when this woman was unconscious, her body in a bath of ice, with no brain wave activity!

What Does This Mean?

These cases challenge man's understanding of life. Even non-religious people are beginning to recognize that "I" am not my body. I merely occupy this body.

But if you are not your body, who are you? Of course, you are more than just a body, but what does that mean? And even more significantly, how can you *live without your body*? If your body dies, what could possibly be left?

The ability to clearly see yourself in a form different than you are in now requires stepping away from the way we normally think. Here is an exercise that may help.

▼

The Biggest Case in Your Life

Imagine you are a lawyer. You've been in practice for ten years, and this is the biggest case of your life. The suit is so significant and the issues so pivotal to the practice of law that the court proceedings are being videotaped. All of the senior partners of your firm are in the courtroom, waiting to see how the case is decided. Yesterday the judge asked you for a brief outlining the key position in your case. He now resumes court, and says in a solemn voice:

"Mr. Goldstein, I have been a judge now for ten years, and I have practiced law for twenty years before that."

Your heart is racing; you have no idea where this is going.

"In all my years on the bench," he continues, "I have never read such a well-organized, lucid, and logically compelling brief as the one you presented. *Mr. Goldstein, you are to be congratulated.*"

And at that moment, the judge and the entire courtroom burst into applause.

If you were to describe your feelings at that moment, I would imagine it would be something like a feeling of elation spreading through your entire being. Intense happiness, awesome joy. Most likely, you wouldn't walk out of court that day; you would float out, feeling like you were transcending time and place. Wowwwwwwwwwwwwwww!

What Part of You Felt It?

The part of you that experienced that sensation wasn't your hands, or your feet, or your head. It wasn't any part of your body that felt it. *You* felt it. *You* felt pleasure. *You* were ecstatic. That sense of pleasure isn't dependent upon your body. In fact, it has no connection to your physical state of being. But y*ou* experienced it.

On the other side of the spectrum, imagine that someone is screaming at you, calling you every nasty name in the book. "You worthless excuse of a human being. I didn't even know that people as low as you could exist." Hearing those words causes you pain. *You* feel hurt. It's not your heart that feels it. It's not your nerves or your synapses that feel embarrassed. *You* do. True, you feel with your fingers, taste with your tongue, and smell with your nose, but it is *you* that experiences it. *You* are the one who occupies the body and controls its destiny. You are the master of the ship.

There are many things that you feel that aren't physical in nature. The full gamut of emotions, from love to hate to rage to jealousy, are things that you feel. You feel proud of your accomplishments. You feel appreciative of kind gestures from others, and you feel hurt by cruel words that people say. It isn't your heart that feels the pain. Euphemistically, we use expressions like a broken heart, but what we really mean is that *you* have been hurt.

You enjoy listening to music and looking at beautiful

landscapes. You feel a sense of awe when you view a majestic mountain. You are moved to tears by the sheer power of the ocean. You are grieved when a friend dies. You are ecstatic when your sister has a baby.

Joy Isn't Physical

Any joy that we experience isn't physical. *Our bodies feel pleasure; our souls feel joy.* Happiness, satisfaction, and serenity — conditions that we value above everything else in life — have little to do with the body. They don't come to us through the body, and they aren't dependent upon our physical state. Most of what makes us human, those feelings and sensations that separate us from the animal kingdom, aren't physical in nature and don't depend upon our body for their existence.

The emotion you feel when holding your newborn daughter for the first time in the delivery room. Can we even describe such an experience? The heart feels it, or more accurately you feel it, but it isn't physical. These are inner conditions that almost defy description. But they are real, and *you* feel them.

When your body dies, *you* will live on. You — with all of your feelings, thoughts, and memories — step out of the coat called the body.

Why Is Death Difficult to Define?

While this may sound pretty straightforward, most of the

world doesn't understand it. Even great thinkers get so lost in the thickness of physicality that they aren't able to distinguish between themselves and the form they temporarily occupy. As an example: one of the great moral debates in medicine today is the definition of death. Is it when the heart stops beating? Is it when there is no brain wave activity? What about a person whose is kept on a respirator in a vegetative coma for ten years? Is he dead or alive?

Death should not be difficult to define. It is when the spirit, the essence of the person, no longer occupies his body. As long as you are housed in your body, you are alive. Once you leave the body, you are dead. What is so complicated about that?

The reason that death is difficult to quantify is because science is very effective at measuring *physical* properties. How long? How dense? How hot? How distant? But *you* are not physical. Your body is physical. *You* aren't. We are so used to mixing ourselves up with our bodies that we have trouble remembering that they are separate entities. And so we end up applying physical measurements to something that *doesn't exist* in that dimension.

It's like trying to weigh light. If someone were to ask you, "How many pounds does that beam of light weigh?" you would give him a strange look. We can measure luminosity. Candle power is a convenient standard of reference. But weight is the wrong criteria to use for measuring light. So, too, we can't use physical attributes to measure *you*. We can't put "the essence of you" into a beaker, add red dye, heat it up, and see what color it turns. The *body* is measurable in physical terms. Blood pressure is quantifiable. Breathing efficiency can be calculated. Gas levels in the blood can be determined. But what test do you run to see if *you* are still there? You aren't physical, and any attempt to measure *you* with physical criteria will fail. And so, just as weight isn't relevant to light, death isn't applicable to you. Death applies to physical life. So while the body dies, you live on.

I Am Not the Brain

There is, however, one more step we need to take to fully grasp this concept. When we begin this process of relating to our body and ourselves as separate entities, many people get a blank look on their faces, these ideas being as foreign to them as moon dust. After a while, though, they start to relate to their bodies as the outer shell, a casing, a tool that they use. Then comes that aha moment. Like a light bulb that clicks on, their faces light up with excitement and they shout, "I get it! I get it! I am not my head. Not my chest. Not my back. I am not even my heart! I finally get it. I am the brain! Right?"

Wrong! When they bury the body, the brain is buried with it. Just as you are not the head or the chest, you are not the brain either. The brain is an organ *you* think with. It is something you use to filter your experiences through, but it isn't *you*. This is a very significant step. *Even your brain is physical.*

A Flash of Intuition

Did you ever have a flash of intuition? It was hard to explain, but you just knew something. Maybe it was a hunch, maybe a thought, but it was there. Then you had to run it through that clunky, concrete process called thought. "Let me see… what I mean is…" This is an example of knowing something and then having to process it through your brain. The brain is sluggish and thick, slow to understand, and quick to forget. When you leave this heavy coat of physicality that we call the body, *you* are no longer limited to thinking through the brain. At that point, everything comes through in a flash of brilliance. *You* perceive. *You* understand. And *you* remember every action, every conversation, and every thought you ever had — from the time that you were an infant until your last dying breath. All right there, accessible, because you and your thoughts are one.

Did you ever wonder what happens to a great Torah scholar who at the end of his days suffers from Alzheimer's disease? He spent a lifetime accumulating Torah knowledge and now can access none of it. What happens after he leaves this earth? As an old man, he is unable to recall the Torah that he learned because the physical organ called the brain isn't functioning properly. His brain is damaged, but he, the essence of him, remembers everything. When he leaves this life, everything will come flowing back.

This tendency to view ourselves as physical entities is a severely limiting thought, and inhibits our growth. On the simplest level, if we don't understand who we are and what we are made of, it is a given that life won't make sense. We will have many, many questions, and there will be no answers.

I Am a Spiritual Being

But even more restricting is that this confusion causes us to view our spiritual experiences as oddities, almost as if they were unnatural. On Shabbos, sometimes we feel spirituality. When we walk into shul on Yom Kippur, maybe we feel holiness. These occurrences feel almost strange because here we are, *physical beings*, having these rare spiritual experiences.

Nothing could be further from the truth! You are not a physical being having an occasional spiritual experience. *You are a spiritual being, temporarily having a physical experience.* You were taken from under Hashem's throne of glory and temporarily put into this body. *You* remain here for but a few years, and then you will return. The same *you*. Not some scaled down version, not some distant cousin. You separate from the body and return, either vastly improved or the opposite… but it is *you*. You are totally, completely spiritual.

This concept is vital toward understanding what Hashem wants from us. One of the reasons that people have trouble relating to certain mitzvos is because they ask, "Why does the Torah harp on such trivia? What does it matter whether I eat this or do that?" From a physical perspective, these questions are valid. If you were just a body, then most of the Torah's mitzvos would not be necessary. There is nothing in the body that is changed by them, so nothing is accomplished. Once we are able to break out of this limited perspective and understand our nature, then much of what Hashem asks from us instantly makes sense. The Torah is the system of *spiritual* perfection. It was hand-crafted by our Maker to guide us toward the heights for which we were created.

Growth in the Spiritual World

Because our bodies exist in the physical world, they are essentially stagnant. Any changes that we make in them are hard-won and quickly lost. Only with great effort can we lose weight. Only with much strain can we build muscle mass. On the other hand, because *we* are spiritual, we are highly susceptible to change. We were put into a situation where our actions, words, and thoughts shape us. They have a profound effect on our essence, and that change remains. And so, we were given the Torah, a program for spiritual success. If we follow that program, we grow level after level, and when we leave this transient state, then forever we will enjoy our accomplishments.

Probably the biggest liability of viewing ourselves as physical beings is that we get so caught up in this world. How much money I make. How much honor I receive. How nice is my car, my house, my boat, my watch. All of these things matter so much because I am here, and it is forever. And even when we discuss such concepts as the World to Come, we tend to look at it as we view travel brochures; they are interesting, but not relevant because we have no intention of ever going there. It won't be me who goes there. I'll be dead. So it just doesn't matter.

But that is the point. It will be you. Not your cousin or some scaled down version of you. *You will step out of this physical body, and you will be exactly what you shaped yourself into.*

Understanding Life

Once we are able to view things from this broader perspective, life takes on a whole new meaning. When we see this world as the gym, and the World to Come as the spa, then how we use our time here matters greatly. If we care

CHAPTER 13

The World Of Peter Pan

> I won't grow up, no I won't grow up. I
> will never wear a tie; no I'll never wear
> a tie. Or a serious expression, not a
> serious expression, In the middle of July,
> in the middle of July. No, I won't grow
> up, never grow up, never grow up. Not I.
> — Peter Pan

One of the results of Hashem putting our holy *nishamah* into a corporeal body is that we are unable to see certain realities. We may be aware of them, but we can't feel them. One of these is our mortality. We have great difficulty seeing ourselves dying. It's not that we don't want to think about death or that the thought makes us uncomfortable. It's much more basic — we just don't intend to die. In our operating mode of thought, it's just not going to happen. Of course, we know that it will occur, but it doesn't enter into our thinking. *Intellectually* we know it, but *emotionally* it remains in some far off place, and we certainly don't live life as if it will ever end.

For example: as a rule, mature people are responsible. They put away money for retirement. They buy life insurance — just in case. They set up annuities for the grandchildren — who aren't even born yet. Everything in life is all planned for. Everything all arranged. Yet somehow, there is one small detail that gets overlooked: what happens after they die?

If dying were a serious possibility, wouldn't you spend time thinking about it? You planned your career. You carefully picked a neighborhood for your family to live in. You were highly selective in choosing schools for your children. When you were sick, you didn't say, "We'll just see what happens." Every part of life was worked out — no stone was left unturned. It's only this one little area you forgot to deal with: the purpose of life and what happens to *me* when it's over.

The reason we don't think about this is that we don't see ourselves ever dying. Of course, on one level we know it. After all, how many people do you know who shook hands with George Washington? How many people can say they met Abraham Lincoln? I may even be able to quote the annual death rate of people in my age bracket by region, but that remains in theory. In the emotional realm, in my real mode of functioning, it will never happen. And we just go on without a care in the world.

A Special Society

The Chofetz Chaim explains that we feel there is a *society* of people who die. It is the older people, the sick people, the unlucky people. They belong to this select group who die — and I am not a member. So while I may be very aware of death, it doesn't apply to me.

Amazingly, this plays out in all times, in all individuals, old or young, healthy or sick. I saw a telling example of this once when visiting my grandmother. In her later years, she would spend the summers in a hotel in the Catskills Mountains.

I would visit regularly, and on one occasion we were sitting together with a number of her friends — all senior citizens. The conversation was pleasant until someone mentioned that "so and so" had passed away. Another person commented, "Oy! What a shame. All of the old people are dying."

I looked around the group and was taken aback. There wasn't a person there under eighty. They were all grandmothers and great-grandmothers. They had all lost their parents. Most had lost siblings. Many had lost a spouse. Yet dying was still a distant concept. It wasn't real. On some level, it remained something that wasn't going to happen to them. It was *the old people* who were dying. The *unfortunate people*. It's a select group — and I am not a member.

Getting Real

This blindness has a real cost. Before a person can think about living with a purpose, he must understand life. And until death becomes real to him, his life remains a never-ending Disney adventure — the world of Peter Pan, where the current situation will last forever, and nothing bad will ever happen. Most of humanity spend their existence in this fantasy world. And much like Peter Pan, in their heart of hearts, each person feels, "I won't grow old. Not I. I will always be young and healthy, and of course, I will never die." And so, like children, they spend their time playing with *things*. Big toys, little toys, trinkets and playthings, castles and moats, bridges and boats, medals of honor and badges of prestige, and of course money, money and some more money. Oh, so luscious and green and crumply. Oh, how happy it makes me!

And while it's true that in this dream world life is cheap and meaningless, it sure is fun! Live it up! You only get one shot at this thing called life — you might as well enjoy it now. Let's party! And the carnival goes on and on and on. Until, they get sick, or old, or infirm or bored, and everything comes to a crashing halt. The party ends. And then the questions begin. Many questions. Real questions. Of course, in their fantasy lives, they were too busy to ask questions. But now, the questions appear. Questions on God. Questions on suffering. Questions that need answers. Questions that have no answers because they are based on a world of make-believe that misconstrues the very reason behind existence.

Amazingly, up until that point, not only weren't there questions, there wasn't even the realization that the celebration would one day end.

Understanding the Master Plan

This phenomenon isn't simply a quirk in human behavior. It is critical to the master plan of Creation. If I could think about my death in a real manner, it would radically change my life. I would be forced to deal with those issues that I currently ignore: *Why did Hashem create me? What is it that I am supposed to accomplish with my life?* These questions would loom so large in front of me that I would have to seek out answers. Those answers would compel me to change.

I wouldn't be able to live in the slumber that I do now. I could no longer spend my time on frivolous pursuits. My *nishamah* would scream out, "*Do something! Accomplish! How can you waste your life like that?*"

Even the body's appetites and desires wouldn't be able to

pull me, as I would recognize that following them damages me. I would view temptations as I do any physical danger. Just as it's obvious that no matter how thirsty I am, I wouldn't drink bleach, so, too, no amount of passion could seduce me to do things that I recognize as self-destructive. And I would ignore the body's foolish demands.

In short, I would live a focused, directed existence, and I would function on a lofty level and achieve great things. But it wouldn't be by choice. I would be forced into it. And that isn't free will. To allow for *practical* free will, both sides have to be equally viable. Living a life of purpose has to be as easy as losing one's way. Thinking has to be effortless as going to "sleep" — getting so caught up in the process of living that I never deal with the most basic of all issues.

The Heavy Cloak of Physicality

To create an even balance, Hashem did more than simply mix desires and drives into man's soul. He placed the *nishamah* into this heavy cloak of physicality that we know as a body. The body acts as covering that prevents the *nishamah* from seeing clearly. The *Mesillas Yesharim* explains that "*Physicality is like the darkness of night to the eye of the mind.*"

One way to envision this is to imagine a cold winter's day. You are waiting at the bus stop all bundled up in your heavy coat, woolen scarf, and thick ski gloves. Your friend asks you for change of a dollar. You reach into your pocket to see if you have four quarters, but you can't feel. Not only can't you feel the difference between a dime and a quarter, you can't even be certain that there are coins in your pocket. There's nothing wrong with your fingers. They didn't suddenly lose their sensitivity; it's just that they are covered with layers and layers of material.

This is similar to the *nishamah* inside the body. The body encases the *nishamah* in a thick outer coating that muffles it. The *nishamah* can't feel because it is covered up with layers and layers of physicality. The result is that man's clear, sharp intellect is dulled. His consciousness is blurred. And at any given time, he is both alert and asleep. Aware and spaced out. And so, he lives in a state of cognitive dissonance, where certain facts that he *knows* intellectually, he just can't feel. They just don't register.

Now, man can be absorbed in the moment, not seeing the future or the consequences of his actions. Now he can live totally in the here and now. And now man is in perfect equilibrium; he can go either way. He has free will — not in theory, but in practice.

Because of this, no matter how obvious it is to others, his end will be hidden from him. Whether he has an IQ of 180 or the intelligence of a gnat, it will be difficult for him to see his death. And that is the critical distinction: *difficult* but not impossible. Man isn't forced to succeed, but success is within his reach. He can go either way. It is in his capacity to just float, never giving more than a passing thought to why he exists, or he can live with meaning and intention and craft a significant life.

Seeing My Death

One of the most effective techniques to living a purposeful life is to concretely deal with death. By confronting death, I am forced to make sense of my existence. I may never completely feel it, but I can touch it. And when I do, it is like a burst of cold air that shakes me out of my slumber. Suddenly, life takes on deep significance. My priorities change. I am no longer satisfied pursuing that which the whole world values, whether it is money, honor, passions or pleasures. I see it for the tin and tinsel that it is. I have a sudden need for meaning and purpose. I need to accomplish significant things. Even suffering begins to make sense, as it fits into a greater plan. The world hasn't changed, but I have.

Hashem created us to grow. He put us into a situation where we will be challenged, and it will be difficult, but He also gave us all of the tools that we need to succeed. The first tool is thinking. Getting out of the world of castles in the sky and dealing with life maturely. Understanding that life is beautiful, but it has a purpose. The first step in this process is recognizing that life has an end. To do this I need to get comfortable with death — my death. Instead of running away from the thought of it, I need to train myself to embrace it. To consciously think about it. While it may not be a comforting thought, this is far and away one of the most powerful techniques for personal growth.

Is Death Depressing?

However, this idea often scares people. They say things like, "I don't want to think about death. It will get me de-pressed. I won't be able to smile again. Wouldn't I be much better off focusing on happy thoughts?" I would like to offer you a very different perspective on this.

Lance Armstrong is one of the most celebrated athletes in the world. Seven-time winner of the Tour de France bicycle race, he is an icon on the stage of the international sports. As much as he is regarded as a competitor, he is respected for his courage — the athlete personifying *true grit*.

Yet his career wasn't a walk in the park. At the age of twenty-one, he was diagnosed with an aggressive form of cancer and given a twenty percent chance of survival. His racing days were clearly over. Much to his doctors' surprise, he survived. While recovering, he began thinking about racing again. Seven years later, he went on to become the second American in history to win the Tour de France, a race known as the world's toughest sporting event. He then went on to win that race seven years in a row, setting a record that may never be broken.

While in the process of setting that record, and then only moderately famous, Lance was interviewed by a reporter about his comeback from cancer. In the course of the discussion, the reporter couldn't help but notice how lightly he seemed to take the disease. Not only wasn't he bitter about the experience, it seemed that he was flippant — maybe even happy about it. At one point the reporter said, "The way that you speak about cancer, it almost sounds like you are glad that it happened."

He replied, "Why would I give up the single greatest thing that happened to me? It made my career. It made my life. Knowing that it could all be over was the most life-changing experience I ever went through. Why would I ever want to give that up?"

A Very Different Perspective

Those are very powerful words and a perspective on death

that few people have.

Thinking about death is depressing — if you don't understand life. If life is a party and death is the end, then death is a downer. If, however, the reason we are here on this planet makes sense, then death isn't depressing; it is a galvanizing, energizing thought. It gets you out of bed in the morning and keeps you moving at night. It gives you the energy to change and to grow. The knowledge that this program is timed adds the sparkle and the luster — almost, if you will, the *fun* — to life. Few things in the world are as dreary as an empty existence, time with nothing to do. Few things make an event as tedious as no goals and no end in sight.

Ironically, the more a person embraces the reality of death, the more he enjoys life. Provided he understands life and how to live it, the thought of the death awakens him and adds spark and vigor to his days. And with it comes a deep sense of balance and harmony. However, a truly mature perspective on life isn't easy to achieve. It doesn't come about by studying some texts and then whamo — everything changes. It requires a change in our emotional makeup, and that takes time, a lot of thinking, and constant reinforcement. And even then, we may have it clearly in front of our eyes at one moment, but then it slips away and we find ourselves again living half asleep.

Came to Paris to Sew on a Button

R' Yisrael Salanter, known as the father of the *mussar* movement, had a student who left Poland and moved to Paris. The word came back to Reb Yisrael that his student, while quite successful in business, was neglecting his religious pursuits. Not long afterward, Rabbi Salanter had occasion to travel to France. When the former student heard about his mentor's arrival, he set out to meet him.

At the train station, when Reb Yisrael disembarked, the student stood anxiously waiting. He greeted his revered teacher, and after exchanging a few civilities, he asked, "What brings the Rav to Paris?"

Reb Yisrael answered, "I need a button sewn onto my coat."

The student was taken aback. *Surely the rabbi didn't hear my question*, he assumed. So he repeated, "What brings the Rav to France?"

Rabbi Salanter answered, "I have heard that there are some fine tailors in Paris, and as I said, I need a button sewn on my coat."

The student said, "Surely there are enough tailors back in Poland that the Rav didn't have to make such a long, difficult trip."

Rabbi Salanter responded, "You can't believe that I would make such a long trip for something as trite as sewing on a button? Yet your soul has made a much longer journey to come to this world, and you live to make money."

The Wake-Up Call

Let's put this into perspective. This student was a mature, successful individual. He had spent his youth growing in spirituality under the guidance of one of the greatest teachers of the generation. He didn't lack any intellectual understanding about the purpose of life. He had studied this subject, delved into it, spent many years involved in it, yet his life no longer reflected that understanding. It wasn't because of questions or doubts that he had, but simply because he got so caught up in the business of living that he lost focus on the reason behind it all.

Reb Yisrael was providing a wake-up call to remind his student of what he knew but was no longer a part of his operating mode. What he was saying was, "I am not here to tell you anything new. These are points that you understand only too well. The problem is that you haven't taken the time of late to dwell on them, to ponder them, and to allow them to shape your behavior and life."

There is a very message to us in this as well. If we would ever be gut-wrenchingly, brutally honest with ourselves and recognize that one day we will leave this earth, that awareness alone would change the whole balance of life. Our *nishamos* would scream out, *"Do something! You only have a short while here. Discover your purpose and pursue it for all you're worth, darn it!"* The result would be a life that is more directed, more passionate, and more meaningful. We would recognize the extraordinary value of life and what we are here to accomplish. And we would be so much more alive, living by design, not by chance. The first step is to be aware of the importance of accepting death. When we do, death becomes something that we embrace, and we find different venues and opportunities to experience it and make it real.

לעילוי נשמת
מאיר בן סנדר הכהן ע'ה

CHAPTER 14

Hello,
This Is My Funeral

Everything that we have discussed until now has been theoretical. A person can read through this entire book and say, "That was very interesting. I have a new perspective on life," and then go right back to living exactly as before.

For these concepts to have any effect on your life, they must become real. It isn't enough to know them. You have to feel them. And that is something that takes a lot of work. To help brings these ideas closer, I want you to try one final exercise.

A Mussar Exercise

Imagine that you find yourself in a large, nicely carpeted

room. There are dark drapes on the wall. The lights are muted; the mood is somber. In the front is a podium where two candles are burning. Gathered are two hundred of your closest friends and relatives. Everyone is seated and listening attentively. All eyes are focused on the front of the room, and there you are, right there in front of everyone — lying in a box. Dead as a doornail. Hello, this is your funeral.

You look around the room, and you see people you haven't seen in years. There's your Aunt Miriam. There's Moshe, your best friend from high school. You want to run over and hug him. In the front row sits your brother. You haven't spoken to him in five years. You want to tell him that you are so sorry for all of those harsh words that you spoke to each other. But you can't. You can't move. You can't speak. You see your cousin Rochel, who you grew up with. She looks terrible; tears streaming down her face. You want to comfort her and tell her it's not so bad. "Come on, Rochel. It happens to all of us."

And you wonder, "Is this real? It doesn't make sense. I can think and see. I know that everyone is in the room. I can even hear them. I must be alive! It must be a mistake. Maybe it's just a dream. That's it. Of course. A nightmare. And when I wake up in the morning, it will all be gone."

You Are Completely Alert

But it doesn't end. Someone gets up to speak and says all sorts of nice things about you. Memories of you when you were younger. Good things that you did in your lifetime. Your rabbi gets up and sings your praises. "Oh, Rabbi," you want to say, "that is so sweet of you. But, really, no need, no need."

You realize, of course, this can't be happening. Not to you. You try to call out, "I want to thank you all for coming. It's been really nice to get together again, but now it's time for all of us to go back home. Okay?" But no words come out of your mouth. Your lips are blue. Your hands are cold.

The unsettling part is that you are alert. You are conscious, but locked in. And… you are scared. Terrified is a better word. Somewhere in the back of your mind, you always knew this moment would come, but not so soon. Not now. I'm not ready. Not yet.

In that one electrifying moment, you come to the realization that life has an end. You finally get it. You finally understand that you were here on this planet for a few short years. You had a mission and a goal, with a particular function to accomplish, and now it is over. You're dead. And you want to scream out, "Stop! This can't be happening. Stop!"

They Take You Out

The ceremony ends. Your friends, the people in your life, come forward. They gather around the coffin, each one putting a shoulder under it. They lift it up. You hear them say, "He was so young." "What a tragedy." "I can't believe it." They carry you out of the funeral home. The crowd, their faces ashen, moves along into the street. They walk till they get to the back of the hearse. Someone opens the door. It swings out slowly, as if it had all the time in the world. They slide the casket — your casket — into the back. Someone comes forward and screws in a metal plate to hold it in place. The crowd begins to scatter. They get into their cars.

You hear the engine start. The hearse pulls out. Through

every bump and twist of the road, you are there. Present. Alert. Aware. You see the highway approaching. The highway you drove on a thousand times. It is so bright and vivid. The sun is shining. It's a beautiful day. "What a nice day for a funeral," you think. But wait. What do you mean? How can this be? And the hearse drives on.

After what seems like an eternity, the hearse arrives at the cemetery. It stops. People get out of their cars. They gather. Someone opens the back of the hearse. You don't recognize him; he is wearing a worn black suit and thin black tie; he looks like he's done this many times before. He says to the others, "Reach in and slide the coffin out." Your old business partner steps forward. "Hey, where are you taking me?" you want to scream out.

It Gets Closer

They slowly pull your casket out of the back. A number of the men take hold of it and start to walk. Slowly. Deliberately. You see your kids. Crying. Trembling. You hear the words, "Abba! Abba!" You want to hug them, but you can't. You want to cry, but you can't.

They carry you to an open grave. You look in. It seems very, very deep. "What are you guys going to do now?" you want to shout. They set the casket down on two wood pieces lying across a deep hole in the ground. They pull the wood away. All that is holding you up are two cloth bands. Men gather on each side and grab the bands. Slowly, they start to lower *you* into the ground. And it hits you. At that moment, the truth comes crashing through. My life. It's over. My life is over! All that I have known it to be, all that I have come to expect — life itself is over. It wasn't supposed to end. Not really. Certainly not like this.

And now the real panic begins. "Stop! What are you doing? This can't be real. Stop it! I am alive! What are you doing? Don't put me in there! I won't be able to get out! Stop! How am I going to breathe in there? Stop! Stop! Stop!"

But they don't stop. They continue to lower you deeper and deeper in. You can no longer see their faces. "Stop. Help! Someone. Please. Please make them stop!" Your mind races a thousand thoughts. How can this be? Life. Life itself. What is happening? You feel a jolt as your casket hits bottom.

They Start Shoveling

Someone picks up a shovel, turns the spade part backwards, and begins dropping dirt. "What are you doing?!" you try to scream. You hear the dirt slam the top of the casket. "Stop!" More dirt hits. The sound is deafening. This wasn't supposed to happen. Not to me. Not yet! More dirt crashes down, and the sound is even louder. "Isn't anyone going to make them stop?! Please! Help! Someone, make them stop!" Again and again, the dirt rains down and it starts to form a layer. "Stop! I am still here. Stop! Stop! Stop!" But it continues. More dirt and more dirt until a layer forms, a complete layer covering your casket. Then it happens.

That moment that you ran from. That one moment that you kept pushing away — not this year. Not now. You knew it had to happen at some point. It was only a matter of time. Maybe later. Some other time. *Now* is that other time. It finally happens. You and your body separate. You go up and your body is left behind in the dirt.

A new wave of terror sweeps over you as one thought occupies your entire being. WHAT COMES NEXT?

In Memory of our grandfather, **Joseph Dworman,** A man of integrity and responsibility. He never compromised when it came to doing what was right, and he never settled for mediocrity. His character and his accomplishments are the legacies he has left us. May the learning and growth that this book inspires, be an Ilui Nishamas **Yosef Aharon ben Baruch Chaim.**   **The Chafetz Family**

CHAPTER 15

WYSIWYG

ספר מסילת ישרים - פרק א

וְאִם יִהְיֶה לְבֶן חַיִל וִינַצַּח הַמִּלְחָמָה מִכָּל הַצְּדָדִין, הוּא יִהְיֶה הָאָדָם הַשָּׁלֵם אֲשֶׁר יִזְכֶּה לִדְבַּק בְּבוֹרְאוֹ וְיֵצֵא מִן הַפְּרוֹזְדוֹר הַזֶּה וְיִכָּנֵס בַּטְּרַקְלִין לְאוֹר בְּאוֹר הַחַיִּים, וּכְפִי הַשִּׁעוּר אֲשֶׁר כָּבַשׁ אֶת יִצְרוֹ וְתַאֲוֹותָיו וְנִתְרַחֵק מִן הַמַּרְחִיקִים אוֹתוֹ מֵהַטּוֹב וְנִשְׁתַּדֵּל לִדְבַּק בּוֹ - כֵּן יַשִּׂיגֵהוּ וְיִשְׂמַח בּוֹ.

Man will acquire perfection and find joy in direct measure to the extent that he conquered his nature and desires; distanced himself from distractions; and attempted to cling to Hashem.

Mesillas Yesharim, Chapter 1

Onkelos the Convert

Printed on the inside of almost every Chumash is the *Targum* of Onkelos. Accepted as one of the most authoritative explanations of the Torah, Onkelos was considered a master of *peshat* (logical understanding). While he was amongst the greatest scholars of his generation, that wasn't how he began.

Born into Roman nobility, Onkelos was the nephew of Titus, the emperor of Rome. Titus was an evil despot, his power exceeded only by his wickedness. He was the one who exiled the Jewish people and destroyed the Bais HaMikdash.

Titus had a sister whose son was Onkelos. Onkelos found great favor in his uncle's eyes and was destined to a life of honor and prestige. However, he began studying the ways of the Jews and recognized the truth of the Torah. The Gemara (*Gittin* 56b) explains that when Onkelos was deciding whether to convert, he wished to consult with his uncle, who was by then dead. He used a form of black magic to communicate with him.

He asked Titus, "Who is important in the World to Come?"

"The Jews," Titus answered.

"I am considering converting," Onkelos said. "Should I join them?"

"Don't do it," Titus answered. "Their religion is far too difficult. You will never be able to keep it. What you should do is fight them. God won't allow His nation to fall to a lowly people. Whoever wages war against the Jews rises to prominence. Battle the Jews and you will ascend to power."

"My uncle," Onkelos asked, "what is your judgment there?"

"Every day they gather my ashes. They judge me. They burn me. Then, they scatter my remains amongst the seven seas."

How Could Titus Give Such Advice?

This Gemara is very difficult to understand. As long as we occupy a body, we are shrouded in darkness. Blinded by physicality, we don't recognize the effects of our actions. But this conversation occurred after Titus left this world. His body was buried, and he was separated from everything physical. He was in the World of Truth.

How could he say something so utterly foolish? He saw

that Hashem rules over the heavens and the earth. He understood that the Jews are Hashem's beloved people. He even mentioned his own punishment for attacking the Jews. Surely the same would await Onkelos if he followed in his uncle's ways. Why would he tell his nephew to fight the Jews?

To answer his question we need a different perspective.

Love Conquers All

If you ask a young *chassan* (a man engaged to be married) what he expects his marriage will be like, most likely, he will answer with a far-off look in his eye. "Oh, it will be wonderful. I will love her, she will love me, and we will live happily ever after."

This same young man may come from a broken home. He may have lived through years of fighting, screaming, and cursing. He may now have a difficult relationship with his parents and siblings, and may have ongoing run-ins with roommates and friends. He may even be aware that he is a difficult person — but it won't matter — his marriage will be harmony and bliss. "*My wife will love me, I will love her, and we will live together in happiness and joy forever and ever.*"

Unfortunately, the divorce courts are filled with such couples. But what went wrong? They started out so in love. He was great. She was perfect. What happened?

What happened was that when they got married, they were infatuated. That infatuation wore off, real life set in, and they weren't ready for it.

Infatuation is like a drug. It affects your senses and changes the way you view things — so everything is wonderful. The whole world is smiling on you. Scientific studies show that falling in love affects the chemistry of the brain in a manner similar to that of cocaine use; the normal balances are changed. A couple "in love" experiences a rush of adrenaline, a sense of euphoria, and the feeling that they will always be happy together. "Her bad habits will never bother me. She will always be tolerant of my being late. We will live forever and ever in this state of bliss." But the infatuation ends.

Infatuation Plays an Important Role

Hashem created infatuation to allow a couple to bond. Men and women have different interests, desires, and value systems. They behave differently, relate to each other differently, and communicate differently. They are so different that you would almost assume that they come from different cultures — maybe even different planets. To ask two individuals who are so dissimilar to live together as one would never work; it would be impossible. To allow marriages to succeed, Hashem put a number of forces into the heart of man — one of them is infatuation.

Infatuation works like sulphur on a kitchen match. When you strike a match against the phosphorous on the match box, it will ignite into a flame. It gets very hot, very quickly. For a second or two, it will flare up, just long enough to light the wood of the match. That flame, however, wasn't designed to last. It was meant to be a catalyst to start the fire, not to keep it going.

Infatuation works the same way. It allows the couple to begin; it starts the process, but they must then do the difficult work of creating a true bond of love. They need to become attuned to each other's needs; they have to learn to actually care about each other, and the hardest part: they have to change those things that bother their spouse. Change isn't easy. Unfortunately, many couples never make the transition.

A big part of the problem is that their initial expectation was unfounded. They walked in thinking, "We are in love, so everything will beautiful and easy. *Love will conquer all.*" The problem is that they weren't in love; they were infatuated. When the drug wore off, they woke up the same people they were before, and then the choice was either change or suffer.

We Don't Fear Death

In a similar vein, most people aren't afraid of death because they have an unrealistic view of what it will be like. Even if they wake up and realize, "I, too, shall die," even if they understand that it won't be my alter ego or my distant cousin, but *me* in the Next World, most people still aren't afraid of death because their image of what it will be like is unrealistic.

Their sense is that it will be all good. I will be an angel in white. All clean. All pure. I will have beautiful wings that sparkle and shine. You will have wings, too. And we will float around together — angels dancing forever and ever in unending glee and joy.

Unfortunately, that isn't what happens.

What happens is that I will be there as I was here. The same me. I don't magically change. I am not transformed into a perfect person. All of those areas of my character that I perfected will be shining bright, and those that I didn't develop will be dull and dark. I remain there as I was here.

In the introduction we discussed WYSIWYG. What You See Is What You Get is an apt parable for what it is like when we leave this earth. When I get there, I will be stripped bare of all of my pretenses and cover-ups. You will see me exactly as I am.

Here I can hide. I am cloaked behind this veil of physicality. I can think one thing and say another — and you won't be the wiser. In the World to Come there is no hiding, no deception. Everything is revealed, out there in the open. I will be exactly what I made myself into. If I spent my time here as a generous, giving person — that is me. If I spent my days being self-serving and selfish, then that is what you will see there. I don't suddenly change into an angel in white. In fact, I barely change at all.

Like a Brilliant Light

The one thing that does change is my clarity of thought. As long as I occupy this body, my mind is blocked. I am enveloped in a thick cloud that shrouds me from truth, and so I see things in distorted ways. *To the eye of the mind, this world is like the darkness of night.*

When I leave this body, the clouds are lifted; my perception is vivid. Like the sun at midday shining bright, everything is illuminated, and I see with a brilliant clarity. I get it. Everything makes sense. I recognize the extraordinary value of time. I realize that I was put on the planet to grow and accomplish. I perceive the immeasurable value of any mitzvah, and the damage wrought with every sin. I fully and completely understand life and why we were created.

Instantly, my value system is changed. All of the things that were once *so* important to me — how much money I had, how much honor I was given, how thick the carpeting in my living room was — I now recognize as trivial. I see all of the trappings of this world as tinsel and glitter. But even though I know that these things are empty, I still hunger for them, much to my own embarrassment.

When Hashem put *me* into this body, the animal soul began as a separate entity. It pulled at me, it tempted me, but it wasn't a part of me. When I give in to it and allow it to rule, not only do I do things that are not in my best interest, those desires become a part of me.

This is a point that many people miss: the drives and desires that I use on a constant basis become a part of me. Initially, they were brought to me by my body, and they were separate from me. But if I gave in to those drives over and over, they melded into my essence. When I leave the body, those desires are still there. My currency and value system are different, but "I" am still the same. And even when the whole concept of the desire no longer applies, the desire remains.

Phantom Pain

This is analogous to the phenomenon of phantom pains. On occasion, people who have lost a limb describe feeling pain in that limb, even though it is gone. The sensation can be vivid. Patients describe a burning pain that shoots through a hand that is no longer there. The appendage is cut off, but the brain hasn't yet made the connection. It receives information that something is very wrong, but the fact that the arm isn't there hasn't registered, so the brain sends out messages of distress, and the person feels pain.

In a similar sense, that is what the World to Come will be like for a person who gave in to his desires on a regular and constant basis; they became a part of him. He no longer has a body, so he can no longer exercise those desires, but the appetite is still there within him.

The Dybbuk Speaking Profanities

An example of this occurred in the times of the Chofetz Chaim when a dybbuk occupied the body of a young woman. A dybbuk is the *nishamah* of a person who has passed away. Because this person sinned so severely, his *nishamah* isn't allowed into the World to Come and is forced to remain in limbo. Under certain circumstances, it is allowed to invade the body of a person who is still alive. When it happened to this young lady, they sent for the Chofetz Chaim to exorcize it.

While waiting for him, some people spoke to the dybbuk. It was clear from the voice and expressions it used that this dybbuk had been a man. One thing that shocked them was the foul language and lewd comments that the dybbuk was uttering. Someone asked it, "Why do you speak that way?"

The dybbuk answered, "That is what I made myself into. That is what I am."

It is almost like what we know as "a dirty old man." Perhaps you have witnessed an old, homeless bum whistling and jeering at each woman that passes him by. He may be too old to perform physically, but he still lusts after women. The desire remains long after the body is no longer capable.

Answer for Titus

This seems to be the answer for Titus. He spent his life immersed in evil, and it became part of his essence. Fighting the Jews was such a factor in his life that it became who he was. He was now in the World of Truth and he understood life, but he was still him.

As foolish as he realized it was, he couldn't change what he had made himself into. It was almost as if he were standing outside himself, wondering how he could utter such foolishness — yet he was not able to stop himself. *"Fight the Jews!"* he screamed, all the while seeing Hashem right there. *"Battle them and you will rise to power!"* he blurted out, feeling an intense sense of embarrassment as all heard his irrational stupidity pouring forth. Yet not being able to control himself, he said it almost against his will.

What Will I Look Like in the World to Come?

Most of us care a lot about the way we look. How many times a day do we check the mirror or smooth out our clothes? These things are very important to us. If a man has a bald spot that he combs over and one day gets caught in a rainstorm, he will suffer great embarrassment when he walks into the office with his hair dripping down. Many women won't be caught outside on a bad hair day. Even a stain on our clothing causes us much distress because "*I look sloppy. I look disheveled, and I am embarrassed.*" We take pride, and rightfully so, in our appearance.

Yet all of these things are external. What about something in my character? What about something that is my very essence? And what if it is ugly? What if all can see it and it is black? As I sit here now, you don't see my selfish streak. What about my temper? Or my laziness? It's covered up. You know me based on my actions. Based on your relationship with me, you take a composite shot of all of my actions and words, and create an image in your mind of who I am. Sometimes you are accurate, and sometimes you are far off, but even if you know a person very well, you can never get it quite right because you are just guessing at what is going on inside him.

What if you could see the real me? What if you could watch my mind as I think? What if you could look into the essence of me as I go through all of those thoughts that my mind spins out in nanoseconds? You would have a very different picture of me. Then, you would see the real me.

No Cover-Up

In the World to Come, that is what you will see. Me. Not my physical self. That part will be buried in the ground. But me, who I really am, exactly as I am, without any touch-ups, for the good or for the bad, disrobed — bare for all to see. Here, I wear this thick coat of a human body, and it covers me up so you can't see me. But when this coat is peeled away and "I" emerge, you will see me stripped of any cover-up, unable to hide behind any facades or rationales. I will be as beautiful as I have made myself… or as ugly.

We were put into this world to mold the "I." That is the sole reason that God created this world: to give us the ability to change, to fashion ourselves. Every situation in life that offers us a choice is part of the molding process. We are constantly being formed. The *decisions* that I make, the *words* that I say, and the *actions* that I take all have their effect on me. They shape me, mold me, and create me into who I will be for eternity.

In this world, we take change for granted. It is a given that a person can start off in one place and with time and effort can become different. All you have to do is will it, and you can make it happen. That is a phenomenon of this world. In the World of Truth, you are what you are. Stuck, frozen in time. In all of Creation, man, and man alone, was given the capacity for growth. No matter how great an angel may be, it always remains exactly the same. The uniqueness of man is his ability to develop. However, that ability has a limit: it lasts only as long as man is in his living state, occupying a body. After the final scene of life is played out, the music stops, the curtain comes down and — *freeze*. That is *you*. In that final pose, you remain forever.

There's Always Time

One of the reasons we take such a cavalier attitude about the World to Come is that we somehow think that what I didn't fix up here, I can always change there. If I didn't quite finish my job, no problem! I can always straighten things out then. And besides it doesn't really matter. We're all alike there anyway, just a bunch of angels in white, shining bright.

While "white" and "shining" may be good metaphors for those who accomplished their mission on the planet, unfortunately, not everyone does. There will be dramatic differences between people there. Some will have reached greatness, and some will not. Some will have come close to perfecting themselves, and others will be mediocre at best. There will be many individuals who are towering giants, shining bright, illuminating the night sky. And there will be others who are diminutive and dull. There will be still others who are pygmies, not even a fraction of who they could have been. And forever they have to live with that — knowing that they could have been so much more. That is one of the most painful experiences that can ever plague a person. That thought may not move us now because we are living in darkness. But then we will understand it only too clearly.

Here is a parable that illustrates this concept.

Frank and Joe

Frank and Joe go way back. They grew up as regular American guys. They were good friends in high school and then roommates in college. Since graduation, they haven't seen each other, but Frank often finds himself thinking back to those old days. Throughout their college years, Frank felt sort of bad for his friend Joe. Joe was a decent guy and all that, but when everyone else was out partying and having a good time, there was Joe the Geek, studying. It seemed that Joe studied morning and night. You almost never saw the guy without a book in his hand. While everyone else was out there getting drunk and having a great time, there was Joe hunched over the books. Poor guy.

After graduating school, Frank and Joe went their separate ways. Joe graduated top in his class, went on to medical school, and became a well-established surgeon. And Frank, well... Frank sort of drifted. He graduated college with straight C's. He never could find a job that he really liked. He works now behind the fish counter in a grocery store.

The Two Meet

As fate would have it, the two meet up many years later when Joe drives into the parking lot of the supermarket. He parks his fancy, imported sports car, steps out and buttons his two-thousand-dollar, custom-made suit. As he walks into the store, who does he see working behind the fish counter? None other than his old friend Frank!

"Frank, old buddy! How you doing?"

"Hey, Joe! Is that you?"

"Wow, Frank. It's been a long time! How are you?"

"Great. I mean... Wow. Joe, you sure look different. Is that a custom-made suit? It sure looks sharp."

"Yeah, just got it. And Frank, you look um... I really like your... um, I mean, your apron."

"Hey, Joe, what you driving these days?"

"Well, I sort of just picked up this new, Italian sports car... And you, Frank, what are you driving these days?"

"Well, I'm driving this old junker, just till I can afford something better."

"Listen, old buddy. Really great seeing you."

"Yeah, you too, Joe. Maybe we'll get together to talk about old times."

"Sounds great. Give me a call."

It Starts to Hit Him

And Frank starts to think. "It sure does seem like his old buddy Joe has it made. He probably works four days out of seven, plays golf two afternoons a week, lives in a custom home, is happily married, and is active in the community. But more than that, he's doing something with his life, something important, something significant. And here I am, thirty-something, working behind the fish counter making little more than minimum wage, driving a beat-up old jalopy, and living in a one-bedroom apartment. Going nowhere."

At that moment, it hits him. "*How could I possibly have been so stupid? What an opportunity I wasted! All those years I used to look at Joe as the loser, and now look at him.*"

But it isn't just at this moment that Frank will bemoan his fate. For the rest of his life, he'll think about it. Every time he scrambles to pay the rent. Every time one of his kids says to him, "*How come so-and-so gets to go on vacation with his parents, and we never go anywhere?*" Every time he wakes up in the middle of the night wondering why he's caught in a dead end job, going nowhere and doing nothing, just wasting away.

For the rest of his life, he will kick himself, and it will always come back to this one realization: "*I blew it.* I had the chance. I could have made myself into something, and I didn't. I could really have been someone, and now look at me. Why? Not for any good reason. I just got caught up in all of the stupid, passing things going on around me. I lost focus on why I was in school in the first place."

Over and over again, the same haunting lyric will play in his mind: "*If only I could go back in time and do it over again.*"

But he can't. He had his shot. He had his one go around,

and it's gone. Now, for the rest of his life, he will be what he made of himself.

The Most Painful Moment in Your Existence

This is a parable to life in the Next World, a parable that is so insightful and powerful that if we take it to heart, it could change our existence. The Vilna Gaon writes that the most painful moment in a person's life is after he leaves this earth. He stands before the Heavenly tribunal, and they hold up a picture for him to look at: a picture of a truly exceptional individual, a person of sterling character traits, who shows intelligence, kindliness, and humility, a person of true greatness, who brought outstanding goodness to the world and changed the very world in which he lived. And they say, "Why isn't that you?"

"Me?! Little me? What do you want from me? Was I some kind of genius? Was I some kind of powerful leader of men? How could I have done those things?"

And they will say one telling line: "That picture is *you*. Not you, as you stand here now. Not you, as you have lived your life. That is you, had you accomplished what you were put on earth for. That is you, had you become what you were destined to be."

At that Moment, You Get It

That moment is the most painful in a person's life. Because at that moment the truth comes crashing through —

you understand what you were capable of doing. You see the purpose of life and recognize what you could have achieved in your stay on this planet. In one flash of recognition, you perceive the greatness of man and what you were capable of accomplishing.

And, it is at that moment that you want to scream out: "Please! Please! Please! Just give me one more chance. Just one more opportunity to spend some time working, improving, changing myself. Please!" But then it is too late. Life is over. This one chance at change, this one opportunity to grow is gone. How you are at that moment in time is how you will be for eternity. And the realization that you could have been so much greater, and accomplished so much more, is the most tragic, heart-rending moment in a person's existence.

The beauty of being alive is that as long as there is breath in your lungs and blood coursing through your veins, you can change and grow. The real value of life is the difference that you can make for eternity. In yourself. In who you will be forever. That is why Hashem put us on the planet, and it is the only thing truly worth striving for.

CHAPTER 16

Two Worlds, One Chance

> ### ספר מסילת ישרים - פרק א
>
> וּמְקוֹם הָעִדּוּן הַזֶּה בֶּאֱמֶת הוּא הָעוֹלָם הַבָּא, כִּי הוּא
> הַנִּבְרָא בַּהֲכָנָה הַמִּצְטָרֶכֶת לַדָּבָר הַזֶּה, אַךְ הַדֶּרֶךְ
> כְּדֵי לְהַגִּיעַ אֶל מְחוֹז חֶפְצֵנוּ זֶה הוּא זֶה הָעוֹלָם.
> וְהוּא מַה שֶּׁאָמְרוּ זִכְרוֹנָם לִבְרָכָה (אבות ד, ו),
> "הָעוֹלָם הַזֶּה דּוֹמֶה לִפְרוֹזְדוֹר בִּפְנֵי הָעוֹלָם הַבָּא".
>
> *In truth, the place of the ultimate pleasure is
> in the World to Come because it was created
> for that purpose. However, the way a person
> gets there is through this world.*
>
> **Mesillas Yesharim, Chapter 1**

In Chapter Eight, we met R' Elazar bar Padas. The Gemara related that when he was unconscious, the rabbis watched as first he *cried*, then he *laughed*, and then a *beam of light* emanated from his head.

Of the three, two are understandable.

The reason that he laughed is clear. If you were told that your portion in the World to Come was equivalent to an estate with thirteen rivers running through it, you would also be quite pleased. The beam of light is also straightforward. When Hashem told him about his reward, he responded, *"That's all? Just thirteen rivers, no more?"* With this, R' Elazar bar Padas demonstrated that he understood his potential. Because of this, he had significant ambitions and aspired for even more. Hashem touched him on the forehead as a sign of approval, as if to say, "Well done. You got it right."

Why Cry?

But why did he cry? Rashi explains that he cried because Hashem told him that he had already lived half of his life. Hearing that half his life was gone caused him such grief that he wept.

This is very difficult to understand. R' Elazar bar Padas had a very hard life. He struggled with poverty, disease, and pain. His lot was so difficult that his first words to Hashem were, "When will my suffering end?" And when Hashem offered him the opportunity to either go back into the life that he had been living or to choose another one, he asked, "Did I already live half of my life?" because he wasn't sure that he had the strength to bear it anymore.

Yet when Hashem said, "You have lived half of your life," he began crying, as if to say, "Oy vey! Half of my life is used up! Woe is me!"

This makes no sense — he should be celebrating! Here he was, living through one of the most formidable challenges imaginable. Every day was a new test that would have crushed a lesser man. Hashem told him that he was doing great. And not only that, he was more than halfway finished. Why should he cry? This was the best news he could have received. It is comparable to a man running a marathon. Just when he passes mile twenty-one, the judges announce that he is on pace to break the world record. The fact that he is more than halfway done the race would bring him great joy. "Just keep it up!" he'd tell himself. Why did Hashem's answer cause R' Elazar bar Padas to cry?

The answer to this question is based on realizing what life meant to him.

When R' Elazar Opened His Eyes in the Morning

R' Elazar bar Padas understood life. He recognized that Hashem put us into this world to give us an opportunity to mold ourselves. We can reach lofty, dizzying heights or we can plummet to the darkest depths. What we will be for eternity is shaped by our actions. And we were put into a position of power — the entire world was created for us and is dependent upon us. If we use our lives properly, we are credited with maintaining the world. If not, it is as if we destroyed it. The stakes are very high.

Because R' Elazar bar Padas saw this so clearly, he opened his eyes every morning with energy, enthusiasm, and drive. He viewed life as a golden opportunity, a treasure to be used, every moment a potential gem that could be his for eternity. Driven by this sense of purpose, he had a deep fervor for life.

Physically, his life was very difficult — so difficult that he wasn't sure that he could continue. But it was precious beyond description. A week, a day, or even a moment of time represented a chance to grow. And so, he loved life. As hard as it was, he cherished it, and hearing that a significant part of his life was used up and gone caused him to cry.

What This Means to Us

There is much that we can take from this. Our lifestyle

today is far grander than that of any other generation. We enjoy liberty and rights that even a hundred years ago were unheard of. Religious tolerance and freedom from oppression are now a given. Technological advancements explode in front of us at a dazzling pace, each one outdoing the one before it. Prosperity and wealth are commonplace. Never in the course of history has so much been available for so many.

That's not the way it used to be. Five hundred years ago life was harsh. Food was scarce, clothing coarse, disease rampant, and marauders were a part of reality. People lived in crowded, unkempt hovels without running water or sanitation. Garbage was thrown onto the street. Bed bugs and lice were ever-present. The average person suffered with hunger and pain, sweltering in the unbroken heat of summer and shivering through the long, frigid winter. Creature comforts were hard to come by.

Those times are gone. Our homes are comfortable, heated, and well-lit. Food and clothing are in abundance. Our streets are paved; our carriages horseless. We no longer chop wood and spend half of our day on tedious chores — everything is ready-made and plentiful. We enjoy remarkable wealth. It would seem that we no longer have any reason to suffer.

We Suffer Today

Yet we do. Materially we have it better than any generation ever did, yet we suffer. But our suffering is of a different type and of a different magnitude. We no longer undergo physical discomforts, we suffer emotionally. We endure heartache, despondency and misery, grief, despair, and wasted lives. We live with a tragic divorce rate and all of the anguish of broken homes. Anxiety, neurosis, personality disorders, obsessions, compulsions, and addictions are as common as the cold. The only recession-proof business today seems to be in the mental health field. There you are guaranteed a steady flow of customers because of the explosion of people in pain. Clinical depression is at an all time high. In the United States alone, over fifteen million people are diagnosed with depression. And that only measures those who suffer so acutely that they can no longer function normally. What about the rest of the spectrum of people who just aren't happy?

Ask someone, "How are you doing?" and you will hear some interesting responses. "Hanging in there." "Surviving." That is a response you would expect from a man who just found out he has terminal cancer and has six months to live. How do you explain it coming from people living in the lap of luxury, enjoying freedom and almost limitless opportunities? *Hanging in there*? *Surviving*?! I don't think it's a mere expression. Rather, it indicates much going on underneath the surface. *Materially*, we are very wealthy, but in measures of joy, happiness, and life satisfaction we are impoverished. We have so much, yet we are so poor.

We Should Enjoy this World

That's not the way that it's supposed to be. Hashem created a custom-made world with flowers and trees, sunrises, and mountain tops for our use. All of the extraordinary beauty was put here for us. The orange, the apple, the pear, and the banana were created for us to enjoy. The flavors, textures, and aromas in food didn't have to be there. Nor did color. Hashem invested great wisdom into creation for our pleasure.

Hashem created the world to share of His good. The greatest gift that we were given is the ability to earn our place in the World to Come, to be close to Hashem. This world is only a passageway. It is a short stopover here; nevertheless, Hashem wants it to be pleasurable. And so this world was built with all of the amenities needed for man to enjoy his stay. It isn't the reason we are here. But it is part of the design.

The reason man can't find happiness is that he isn't focused on why he was created. Assuming that this world is the end all and be all of Creation, man pursues everything but what he was put here for, and so he lives out of sync with his very nature. Then, for some "strange reason," nothing seems to satisfy him. So he begins that elusive search for happiness — in all the wrong places.

I'll Be Happy When...

Like a mantra, people utter the words, "I will be happy when..." Each person has his own fill-in for the blank, but whatever it is, his happiness depends on it. *It* might be the newest car, the fanciest house, the corner office, or the wardrobe worth dying for. *It* could be the right spouse, acceptance into medical school, that great job, or people who understand me... Each person has his own value system and his own criteria, but he clearly knows, "Once I get *it*, I will finally be happy."

Yet an amazing thing happens. He does finally get *it*! And lo and behold, he still isn't happy. What happened? It was all that he needed. It was all that he wanted. He finally has it. Why isn't he satisfied? What is the problem?

The problem is that he isn't living the way his life was

planned. If you use a fine surgical instrument to pry open a window — it does a lousy job, and it ruins the blade. When you live in a way other than your Creator intended, life just doesn't work well. And slowly, after a lifetime wasted, you learn that money doesn't fill your soul. Pleasure and honor just don't satisfy your inner needs. Oh, they look so alluring. They exert this almost magical pull, but they never work. At the core of your essence, you remain empty. And like drinking when you are hungry, as soon as the excitement of finally getting *it* passes, you find yourself more unsatisfied than before. Unfortunately, most people discover this way too late in the game to do anything about it.

—————▼—————

The Most Enjoyable Activity Is Growing

Hashem created the human to grow. It is in his very nature. Growth is the activity that brings him the most joy. Hashem put man into this world with many challenges and much to accomplish. When man uses his life appropriately, he achieves inner balance and harmony; he is at peace with himself. The sun is shining bright. The birds are chirping. The colors are so vibrant — he is so alive. He is happy. When he uses his life for any other purpose, he finds himself empty and unsatisfied, listless, with a constant need to fill a void within.

This is one of the great ironies of life. The more a person focuses on purpose and meaning, the more bountiful is his life. The more he focuses on taking in all of the *pleasures* this world has to offer, the less he enjoys them. *Eat, drink and be merry for tomorrow we may die* is a formula for finding less pleasure and less enjoyment in life. The hedonist is bound to fail because his existence becomes just an endless race to fill an ever widening gulf within. This isn't a quirk in the system, and it isn't by accident. It is part of the design.

Make no mistake, pleasures have their place — they are *tools* to be used. When a person is content, he is better able to serve his Creator. By properly using the luxuries and comforts of this world, man elevates himself. He transforms the mundane into the holy and is better suited for his mission. By doing this, he also elevates the world itself because he is using it for its intended purpose. He enjoys this world and gains the World to Come.

The Five-Star Hotel Called Life

We are in this hotel called life for but a few short years. Nevertheless, Hashem designed it as a five-star accommodation with many luxuries and amenities. The difficult part is not losing our way, not mistaking the passing for the permanent, the hotel for our home.

Within us, Hashem placed a regal *nishamah*. It is the princess that is accustomed to living in lofty heights. Because it can't be satisfied with living a shallow, empty existence, it can help us chart our course. It is the voice inside that screams out, "Accomplish! Grow! Do something meaningful with your life." And it finds no satisfaction from anything in this world, because it comes from so much higher. That voice inside speaks to us. We need to train ourselves to listen.

The challenge of life is to perfect ourselves by finding the path that brings about our growth, allowing our inborn desires to do what is right to win out. The tricky part is that Hashem married the princess to the peasant, putting my holy *nishamah* into this thick body. So now it is *I* who is in contradiction. *I* want to grow, yet *I* want to mire in the mud. *I* want to shoot for the stars and reach the heights of greatness, and *I* am satisfied to go on living without a plan and without direction, just taking life as it comes.

The situation is complex because we are presented with many difficult tests in life. This world is the gym. We were born into a set generation, given a certain amount of intelligence and talent, and put into an exact life. The situations are insignificant. They are but props — stage settings — that we were given to act out our role. At the end of my days I will be judged, but not as compared to you — I will be shown an image of me. And they will say that one most telling line, "That is you. That is you had you lived your life as you could have... as you should have."

The Torah, the System of Spiritual Perfection

To help us find our path, we were given very clear directions. Hashem gave us the Torah, the guidebook for life. Written by our Creator, it contains all of the wisdom of the universe. It serves as the system for spiritual perfection and is a beacon that guides us through the darkness of this world. Our mission is to discover it, to seek it out. If we haven't had the life's opportunity to study it sufficiently, we need to find someone who can teach us, someone who is learned in its ways and can show us how to apply it to our particular circumstances.

Actively creating a meaningful, productive life may at times seem daunting. It requires thinking. It often demands breaking out of given molds and accepted behaviors. And a person may feel, "How can I do this? How can I find my way amongst the many paths in front of me?"

Rambam — Lightning Flashes

In the *Guide for the Perplexed*, the Rambam writes that most of the *Nevi'im* (prophets) didn't have regular divine revelations. Some had them intermittently, some had them rarely, and many had a single experience. Yet the experience shaped their lives because at that moment, they saw the truth with brilliant clarity. It was like a lightning flash that lit up the night.

To better understand what the Rambam means, imagine a man lost in the woods. He has been walking aimlessly for days. No matter how he tries, he can't find his way back home. His mood turns from bad to worse when it starts to rain. Determined, he plods on, until finally, he stumbles and falls to the ground. In desperation, he raises his eyes to the heavens and cries out, "Hashem! Please help!" Suddenly, as if on cue, a lightning bolt bursts across the sky and lights up the darkness. In that single flash, the entire forest is lit up and he is able to see his village. "There it is. I see it! Thank You, Hashem!" he exclaims. The vision was momentary, but it was enough. He is no longer lost. It may take him days to travel, but he knows the way.

That is life. We are lost in a sea of desires, temptations and distractions. Amidst a life that is very confusing, we have flashes of understanding, certain moments when we get it. Maybe it's at a funeral, maybe at a joyous occasion, or maybe on Yom Kippur in shul. At that instant we see things clearly.

That is the moment to make life decisions. That clarity will shortly escape, but if you use it to guide your life's course, you'll know that you are headed in the right direction.

Two Worlds, One Chance

We were put into this world given almost unlimited potential, and challenged with making ourselves great. We were given one shot at life. What we make of it is what we are for eternity. The ways of the Torah are pleasant, so the passage, while taking courage and fortitude, is enjoyable. When a person follows the Torah's ways, he gains two worlds. Living a meaningful, fulfilling life, he acquires this world and the World to Come. When he chooses otherwise, he loses both. Two worlds. One chance.

May your journey be successful.

Ben Tzion Shafier
Tu B'Av 5770

Where Do We Go From Here

I hope that you have found this book meaningful. While it offers information, its primary purpose is to impart a perspective – a perspective that should be the underpinnings of everything that we do. If this book brought you to think about the big issues of life, then I consider it a success — it has done its job. The question is: where do we go from here? How do you maintain that perspective? How do you apply it to your life? What is the next step?

Certainly, there is no one answer, as this is one of the great challenges of life. To deal with this issue, a wealth of material has been developed by Torah giants over hundreds of years. The difficult part is accessing that material. Many people find applying the Mussar works a daunting task, one that just doesn't seem to work for them.

A tool that I would like to suggest is "The Shmuz." The Shmuz is exactly what the title implies, a mussar "talk" that deals with a wide range of subjects: davening, emunah, bitachon, marriage, parenting, people skills, working on anger, jealousy and humility.... At this point, there are over two hundred lectures, and the list is growing. Similar in style to the book that you have just read, the Shmuz takes the Torah sources and applies it to life – to your life in the twenty first century.

The lectures are available in a number of portals, and one is the Shmuz.com. There you can listen, watch, read, download or podcast. I welcome you to look around the site. You will also find many other shiurim and materials there.

If you are from an earlier age, or if you try to avoid internet usage, there are still a number of ways to access the Shmuz. We have CDs of the audio, books on various topics, and you can listen to the Shmuz on Kol Halashon.

If you would like more information or would like to bring the Shmuz to your community, please call the Shmuz office at 1- 866-613-TORAH (8672). I also welcome any thoughts or comments. You can reach me by e-mail me at rebbe@ theshmuz.com.

Following this page, is a listing of the Shmuzin.

LISTING OF SHMUZIN AVAILABLE AT THESHMUZ.COM

Shmuz #1
Eternal People

Shmuz #2
Yomim Noraim – Issues of the Day

Shmuz #3
Yom Kippur – The power of Teshuvah

Shmuz #4
Appreciating Olam Hazeh

Shmuz #5
Appreciating our Wealth

Shmuz #6
Its not Geneivah, it's Shtick

Shmuz #7
Noach: Understanding Belief

Shmuz #8
Power of Prayer

Shmuz #9
Akaidas Yitzchak

Shmuz #10
Questioning G-d: Finding and keeping your Bashert

Shmuz #11
Kibud Av of Eisav – Appreciating Parents

Shmuz #12
People of Principle

Shmuz #13
Free Will – Part 1: Nefesh Habahami, Nefesh Hasichli

Shmuz #14
Living like a Rock

Shmuz #15
Chanukah G-d fights Our Wars

Shmuz #16
Olam Habba: The Greatest Motivator

Shmuz #17
Acquiring Olam Habba The Easy Way – "Everyone needs a Mike"

Shmuz #18
Difference Between Emunah & BitAchon – 4 Levels To Emunah

Shmuz #19
Free will - Part 2: I Never Do Anything Wrong

Shmuz #20
Davening - Making it Real

Shmuz #21
Choosing a Career

Shmuz #22
Evolution - Does it Make Sense?

Shmuz #23
I'll never die. Not me. No way.

Shmuz #24
Understanding Life Settings

Shmuz #25
They don't make anti Semites like they used to

Shmuz #26
Loshon Horah – Squandering our Olam Habbah

Shmuz #27
Respecting the Institution – America the Beautiful

Shmuz #28 People Believe what they want to Believe

Shmuz #29
The Busy Generation

Shmuz #30
Anger Management

Shmuz #31
The Voice Inside

Shmuz #32
Understanding Nature – Putting the "WOW" back into Nature

Shmuz #33
Where Was G-D During the Holocaust?

Shmuz #34
Israel: Exalted Nation / Oppressed People

Shmuz #35
Hashem and Man: Master and Servant (Understanding Humility)

Shmuz #36
For the Love of Money

Shmuz #37
Three Types of Miracles – The Fifth Level of Emunah

Shmuz #38
Where is Hashem – The Sixth Level of Emunah

Shmuz #39
I Need, Needs

Shmuz #40
Acher – The Importance of Torah – Founding an Organization

Shmuz #41
Rebbe Akiva and Rochel – Potential of the individual

Shmuz #42
Tricks of the Soton

Shmuz #43
Soton out of the Box

Shmuz #44
Bar Kamtza - Do you really have Free Will?

Shmuz #45
WYSIWYG-Developing Willpower

Shmuz #46
Greatness of Man- Beyond our understanding

Shmuz #47
Cognitive Re-structuring

Shmuz #48
Being a Nice Guy

Shmuz #49
Yom Kippur- The Capacity of a human

Shmuz #50
Bitachon – Learning to Trust HASHEM

Shmuz #51
Bitachon part II- Bitachon & Hishtadlus – Finding the balance

Shmuz #52
Bitachon Part III- The Maaser Shmuz

Shmuz #53
I Hate Criticism

Shmuz #54
Understanding Laziness

Shmuz #55
Staying Pure in an Impure World

Shmuz #56
Chanukah – The Death of Right and Wrong

Shmuz #57
Torah – Creating Worlds

Shmuz #58
Arrogance – Misdirected "Greatness of Man"

Shmuz #59
Humility – An Issue of Perspective

Shmuz #60
Tidal Waves and Middas HaDin

Shmuz #61
Heroes!

Shmuz #62
Plan Your Life, Live Your Plan

Shmuz #63
Davening – Close Encounters with our Creator

Shmuz #64
Davening Part II- The Love of a Father To A Son

Shmuz #65
Davening Part III- The Third System – The Power of the Words

Shmuz #66
Torah – The Mark of the Man

Shmuz #67
Understanding and Eliminating Jealously

Shmuz #68
People Skills

Shmuz #69
Yitzias Mitzraim – A War of Ideology

Shmuz #70
Onah – The Torah's Sensitivity to another's pain

Shmuz #71
Chesed: Being Like HASHEM

Shmuz #72
Respect : The Students of Rebbe Akiva

Shmuz #73
Self Respect;
The Basis of
it All

Shmuz #74
Divaykus in
Our Times

Shmuz #75
Respect :
The Students
of Rebbe
Akiva-The Art of
Appreciation

Shmuz #76
Asking Advice

Shmuz #77
Man-Based
Morality

Shmuz #78
Kiddush
HASHEM

Shmuz #79
Reward &
Punishment

Shmuz #80
It's Never Too
Late

Shmuz #81
All for my
People

Shmuz #82
Why Me? Un-
derstanding
Suffering

Shmuz #83
The Moon was
Jealous- Under-
standing the
Forces of Nature

Shmuz #84
Why Me?

Shmuz #85
MOTIVA-
TION!

Shmuz #86
To Tell the
Truth

Shmuz #87
Self Control!

Shmuz #88
Chanukah
- The Effect
of Outside
Influences

Shmuz #89
Malbin Pnei
Chavero

Shmuz #90
Torah
L'Shmah

Shmuz #91
I Never
Forget

Shmuz #92
TACT

Shmuz #93
Shabbos-
Foundation of
our Emunah

Shmuz #94
On Being
Judgmental

Shmuz #95
Time Man-
agement

Shmuz
#96 Purim
III-Sieze the
Moment

Shmuz #97
Living the
Good life

Shmuz #98
The Power
of Positive
Thinking

Shmuz #99
Men are from
Mars

Shmuz #100
Keeping The
Dream Alive

Shmuz #101 -
Why Pray?

Shmuz #102
Learning
To Love
HASHEM

Shmuz #103
Torah Study
- The Key To
It All

Shmuz #104
Parenting 101

Shmuz #105
- Understand-
ing Life Set-
tings PART II

Shmuz #106 -
The Power of
a Tzibbur

Shmuz #107 -
CHAZAK!

Shmuz #108
- Servant of
HASHEM

Shmuz #109 - ACHLOKES! The Damage of Conflict

Shmuz #110 - Becoming a Great Individual

Shmuz #111 - Sustaining Spiritual Growth

Shmuz #112 - Chesed - The Essense of Judaism

Shmuz #113 - Tshuvah - Two Elements to a Sin

Shmuz #114 - Creating a Balanced Self Esteem

Shmuz #115 - Preparing For Yom Kipper

Shmuz #116 - GROWTH

Shmuz #117 - Optimism

Shmuz #118 - Da'as Torah

Shmuz #119 - Bris Milah

Shmuz #120 - Thrift

Shmuz #121 EMES The Whole Truth

Shmuz #122 - Parenting 102

Shmuz #123 - Chanukah: Whose Side Are You On?

Shmuz #124 - Life is Like a Box of Chocolates

Shmuz #125 - Business Ethics

Shmuz #126 - Dignity of Man

Shmuz #127 - Breaking The Forces Of Habits

Shmuz #128 - Kiruv: The Message & The Medium

Shmuz #129 - HaKaras HaTov: Recognizing the Good

Shmuz #130 - Living With Bitachon

Shmuz #131 - Working For A Living

Shmuz #132 - PURIM: Being Human

Shmuz #133 - ReJEWvinate

Shmuz #134 - PARENTING 103: Setting Limits

Shmuz #135 - Imagination: The Devil's Playground

Shmuz #136 - I'm Never Wrong

Shmuz #137 - Being Sensitive

Shmuz #138 - The Potential & The Present

Shmuz #139 - The Power of Speech

Shmuz #140 - The Arabs and The Jews

Shmuz #141 - Parenting Part IV: Sibling Rivalry

Shmuz #142 - The Power of Laughter

Shmuz #143 - Stages of Change – Part 1: Denial

Shmuz #144 - Stages of Change Part II: Support Groups

LISTING OF SHMUZIN AVAILABLE AT THESHMUZ.COM

Shmuz #145 - Stages of Change Part III: Taking Action | Shmuz #146 - The Impact of One Mitzvah | Shmuz #147 - Finding G-d | Shmuz #148 - Rich, Richer, Richest - How to be Wealthy | Shmuz #149 - The System of Tshuvah | Shmuz #150 - Being a Religious Atheist

Shmuz #151 - Be Brave, Be Bold | Shmuz #152 - In G-d's Image | Shmuz #153 - Marriage: A Work in Progress | Shmuz #154 - Marriage: A Work in Progress PART II | Shmuz #155 - Chanukah - Flexi-dox Judaism | Shmuz #156 - Get Out of Debt

Shmuz #157 - Learning to Love Learning | Shmuz #158 - Me & My Big Mouth | Shmuz #159 - 212 Degrees - Just One Degree Hotter | Shmuz #160 Purim: Sheep to the Slaughter and Concert Bans | Shmuz #161 April 15th: The Test of Emunah | Shmuz #162 Learning to Care

Shmuz #163 Only the Good Die Young | Shmuz #164 I Hate Criticism | Shmuz #165 The Art Of Listening | Shmuz #166 Everybody is doing it | Shmuz #167 - Sefiras Ha'Omer Countdown to Ka'balas Ha'Torah | Shmuz #168 Emunah

Shmuz #169 Anger Taming the Monster Within | Shmuz #170 Sweet Revenge | Shmuz #171 Don't Sweat the Small Stuff | Shmuz #172 - The Tisha B'Av Shmuz | Shmuz #173 - Children of HASHEM | Shmuz #174- The Illusion of Reality

Shmuz #175 - Rosh Hashana Prep - Yom Ha Din | Shmuz #176 - Tshuvah Shmuz 5769 - A Diamond with a Flaw | Shmuz #177 - Being Grateful | Shmuz #178 - To one person you may be the whole world | Shmuz #179 - The Commitments of a Jew | Shmuz #180 - Why We Want Mosiach Now

LISTING OF SHMUZIN AVAILABLE AT THESHMUZ.COM

Shmuz #181 - Emunah in Difficult Times

Shmuz #182 - Tolerating Evil: A Perspective on Recent Events

Shmuz #183 - With Perfect Faith: Bitachon in Turbulent times

Shmuz #184- The Galus Mentality

Shmuz #185 - Responsibility

Shmuz #186 - G-d for the Perplexed

Shmuz #187 elf Mastery- The Key to Good Middos

Shmuz #188 - Rich Man Poor Man - The Ferris Wheel of Life

Shmuz #189 - Encounters with G-d

Shmuz #190 - My Rebbe

Shmuz #191 - Combating Robotic Judaism

Shmuz #192 - HASHEM really cares

Shmuz #193 - A Clash of Civilizations

Shmuz #194 - Tisha B'Av- What we can do to bring the Geulah

Shmuz #195 - Stop Playing G-d!

Shmuz #196 I'd be the first to Thank HASHEM if

Shmuz #197 - Teshuvah Shmuz 5770 - Limiting Beliefs

Shmuz #198 - Life Transforming Moments

Shmuz #199 - Lashon Harah- Mindless Chatter

Shmuz #201 - Chanukah - The Power given to Man

Shmuz #202 - Outcomes and Intentions

Shmuz #203 - Disney Land USA, the ADD Generation

Shmuz #204 - Listening to your messages

Shmuz #205 - The Giant Within

Shmuz #206 - Teshuva Shmuz